GREASED L

FOR S

C000152666

GREASED LINE FISHING FOR SALMON

Compiled from the Fishing Papers of the late
A. H. E. WOOD, of Glassel,
by
"JOCK SCOTT"

With contributions by
The Rt. Hon. J. W. HILLS, P.C.
&
G. M. La BRANCHE

ANDRE DEUTSCH

To the Memory of
The late A. H. E. WOOD, of Glassel

A Master of his Craft

First published 1935

Reprinted 1984 by André Deutsch Limited
105 Great Russell Street London WC1

Copyright © 1935 by D. Rudd
Introduction copyright © 1984 by Antony Atha

ISBN 0 233 97734 1

Printed in Great Britain by
Ebenezer Baylis & Son Limited
The Trinity Press, Worcester and London

FOREWORD

The publication of *Greased Line Fishing for Salmon* in 1935 marked a watershed in the techniques and methods whereby people fished for salmon in the summer months of the year. Before Wood, the traditional sunk line, albeit with smaller flies, was the rule; after Wood all was changed.

There had been light line and small fly specialists who had written of summer fishing before, Chaytor and Crosfield to name but two, but neither of these two great anglers nor anyone else had made the ultimate leap forward. So Wood's 'discovery' of greasing the line to keep the fly just under the surface film must rank in angling terms with Skues's introduction of the nymph to its rightful place in the chalk streams.

Wood has his detractors and the gospel according to Wood as outlined by 'Jock Scott' has been questioned. Rightly so, in my opinion, but I also think that much of the confusion has arisen because Wood's teachings were misinterpreted and insufficient allowance made for the basis from which Wood drew his conclusions. First of all Wood was in a funny way a very *inexperienced* salmon fisher. He caught, so we read, no fewer than 3,540 salmon in his lifetime but only 50 of these fish were *not* caught at Cairnton on Dee. We are told he disliked wading and certainly he fished from the bank with a single-handed 12½ foot rod. This was fine at Cairnton where the fish all lie under the Cairnton bank, but it did mean that he had to cast square across the river to reach the furthest lies. He therefore had to mend his line because if he had not then little of his water would have been fished properly. So, simply because Wood, perforce, fished his own water in that way, it became the way to fish. Again, the Dee in the years 1913-35 was the spring river *par excellence* with large numbers of free-taking fish. Given those fish, it is understandable that Wood felt that salmon 'never deliberately came short'. Wood hardly ever fished after the end of May but if he had, and if he had had a wider and more varied experience of salmon fishing, he would no doubt have thought differently and probably fished differently.

In this respect he was, I think, ill-served by his amanuensis 'Jock Scott', particularly in the famous or infamous table of comparisons between sunk line fishing and greased line fishing which is not only preposterous in its claims but in practice quite irrelevant.

Neither Wood nor 'Jock Scott' realised what Wood's method of presenting the fly on a greased line achieved. Fished in this way the fly imitates, as far as the angler can make it, the action, or rather inaction, of plankton, one of the staple foods of the salmon in the sea, which hangs inert in the current. This is a perfectly legitimate and worthwhile tactic in the summer when the water temperature rises above 48°F and is generally most successful when the water temperature is even higher. The fisherman must fish his fly as slowly as possible, constantly mending the line to slow down the pace at which the fly crosses the river. When fishing like this the fisherman is not in direct touch with his fly, so he must give line when the fish takes and give the salmon plenty of time to take the fly down before tightening. This is the basis of the striking/non-striking controversy which has arisen out of this book.

If, on the other hand, the angler is imitating a small fish, either on a sunk line in the spring or on a greased line in the summer, he will, if he is fishing correctly, be in direct touch with his fly and should strike immediately he feels his fish. Wood himself was a confirmed striker as is apparent in his comments throughout this book.

There are other examples of this type of misinterpretation in the book, but in spite of these it remains a major book on salmon fishing. It chronicles a change in the way fish are caught in the summer and it is full of the most penetrating observations on fish and fishing. All salmon fishermen owe 'Jock Scott' a great debt for his work and his writing, and all of them who have not read it will become better and wiser fishermen for having done so.

Antony Atha

PREFACE

A WORD as to the origin and purpose of this volume. For a number of years prior to his death, the late Mr. A. H. E. Wood had been collecting material with a view to publishing a book on the method of salmon angling which he invented. In September, 1933, he discussed this proposed book with me; giving me a rough outline of the form it would take. He proposed that his chapter in the *Lonsdale Library* volume on *Salmon* should form the hub around which the book should be built; that a section should be devoted to questions and answers, and that the remainder should be compiled from his notes and records.

Thanks to the kind offices of his son, Captain E. G. Wood, to whom I—and all salmon anglers—owe a debt of gratitude for allowing me access to his late father's papers, I have been able to compile the present volume, which will, I venture to hope, be found both interesting and helpful to the greased line fisherman. Wherever possible, I have quoted Mr. Wood word for word, as I feel sure that his large circle of friends would wish to read his own views expressed in his own way.

viii   PREFACE

The opinions of such a well-known and successful angler cannot fail to interest and instruct, even though, in some ways, they may conflict with the old-established principles of salmon fishing. Mr. Wood has said, " I never try to cram greased line down anyone's throat," and personally I should like to make it clear that I echo this remark.

While enthusiastic for the greased line technique, I most emphatically do *not* say that it is the only method worth using. My object in compiling this volume is to make converts; not to hurl sneers at the older-established methods. To do so would be not only unwise, but downright stupidity; for are not hundreds of salmon caught by sunk-fly, minnow and prawn? That the greased line is a more deadly method I firmly believe; and that it is extremely interesting, instructive and artistic there is no doubt whatsoever, and there I will leave it.

I have felt that Mr. Wood's remarkable abilities should be commemorated in a book; that he should have a volume entirely devoted to himself and his method. Hitherto his revolutionary practices have been described merely in chapters of books devoted to salmon fishing as a whole, and to my mind, that is not enough. I offer the present volume, therefore, as a tribute to the memory of a very great fisherman.

Mr. Wood was no arm-chair-angler; he was essentially the practical fisherman, and his motto was, " the proof of the pudding is the eating of it." How successful he was, a study of the chapter devoted to the Cairnton records will show. Again, if asked a question, his reply usually commenced, " Well, in my experience. . . ." There you have, in a nutshell, his attitude towards the sport. He was no theorist, and when assailed with argument, based his replies upon practical experience.

Undoubtedly, the qualities which most impressed one were his enthusiasm and observation. Few fishermen can have equalled him in keenness, and very few in the powers of observation and deduction ; which, coupled with great manual dexterity in the handling of rod and line, were, I think, the reasons of his extraordinary success.

Although, in later years, salmon fishing was undoubtedly the favourite sport, Mr. Wood was far from being a man of one hobby. He was, or had been, a good long-distance swimmer, a fine shot at fur or feather, a yachtsman, a most enthusiastic gardener and an expert bee-keeper. After, or perhaps even before, his fishing came his gardens at Glassel and Cairnton. The former, indeed, were wonderful examples of what can be accomplished by hard work and enthusiasm ; and they were well known to many gardening experts. Rockeries and lawns alike showed evidence of unremitting care and attention.

I once asked Mr. Wood whether, in the event of his fishing being at its best during the height of the gardening season, he would neglect the former for the latter, or *vice versa*. He did not seem able to give a decided answer ! As he said, " I have so many irons in the fire that I always seem to be on the go."

My best thanks are due to all those who have helped me in the compilation of this book : to Mrs. E. M. Crosfield, who kindly gave me permission to publish the late Mr. Ernest Crosfield's letters to Mr. Wood ; to Captain E. G. Wood for his permission to publish matter taken from his late father's papers, and for much very valuable assistance ; to the Right Honourable J. W. Hills for his delightful contribution (Chapter I) ; to Mr. G. M. La Branche for permission to include the correspondence between himself and Mr. Wood, and for his contribution to Chapter IX.

To the following kind lenders of photographs : Mrs. E. M. Crosfield ; Messrs. J. Arthur Hutton, and Eric Taverner.

To Messrs. Hardy Bros., Ltd, who kindly tied flies for reproduction in the frontispiece ; and to Mr. L. Kilroy, who supplied replicas of the unique new patterns which Mr. Wood invented ; to Messrs. Seeley, Service & Co. for the loan of blocks.

Never, surely, has an author received more kind and generous support, often given at great personal inconvenience and trouble, and I am very grateful. So, I feel sure, will be my readers.

J. S.

LIST OF CONTENTS

CHAPTER   PAGE

I. A. H. E. Wood: an Appreciation, by
   J. W. Hills   17

II. Tackle   27

III. Mr. Wood's Casting Methods . .   54

IV. Greased Line Fishing
      I. first principles   63
      II. the birth of the idea . . .   69
      miscellaneous tips   108

V. Asked & Answered   119

VI. Sunk Fly   148

VII. The "Wood" & "Crosfield" Methods
     Compared   162

VIII. The Cairnton Records   179

IX. The Dry Fly at Cairnton . . .   201

Index   217

LIST OF PLATES

PLATE

1. FLIES FOR USE WITH THE GREASED LINE   INSIDE COVER

                                                                   FACING PAGE

2. PLAYING A FISH 62
        Photo : J. Arthur Hutton.

3. THE SALT VATS 62
        Photo : J. Arthur Hutton.

4. A FISH JUST HOOKED . . . 63
        Photo : Eric Taverner.

5. KELPIE 63
        Photo : J. Arthur Hutton.

6. A. H. E. WOOD CASTING . . . 94
        Photo : Eric Taverner.

7. A GOOD DAY AT CAIRNTON . . 94
        Photo : J. Arthur Hutton.

8. WAITING FOR A RISE . . . 95
        Photo : J. Arthur Hutton.

9. THE RIVER AT WADING HEIGHT . 95
        Photo : Eric Taverner.

10. A CAIRNTON SALMON . . . 158
        Photo : Eric Taverner.

11. "IN HIM!" 159
        Photo : J. Arthur Hutton.

xiii

FACING PAGE

12. THE GHILLIE SHOULD BE KEPT OUT OF SIGHT   159
       Photo : J. Arthur Hutton.

13. THE LATE MR. ERNEST CROSFIELD WITH ONE
       OF HIS TROPHIES   190
       Photo : Mrs. Crosfield.

14. THE FINISH OF A " MEND "   .   .   .   190
       Photo : Eric Taverner.

15. SALMON SCALE   191
       Photo : J. Arthur Hutton.

16. SALMON SCALE   191
       Photo : J. Arthur Hutton.

LIST OF TEXT ILLUSTRATIONS

FIGS.   PAGE

1. CASTING WITH UPRIGHT RINGS 33
   CASTING WITH OSCILLATING RINGS . . . 33

2. THE CAIRNTON CARD 39

3. SINGLE CAIRNTON 51
   DOUBLE CAIRNTON 51

4. MR. WOOD'S CASTING METHODS . . . 55

5. SUNK FLY (left) COMPARED WITH GREASED LINE . 65

6. A FISH WHICH MISSES THE FLY . . . 67

7. THE RESULT OF CASTING ACROSS A FAST CURRENT
   INTO AN AREA OF SLOWER WATER AND LEAVING
   THE LINE TO LOOK AFTER ITSELF . . . 72

8. CAST TO 1. THE CURRENT ACTS ON THE LINE AND
   2 IS FORMED. LIFT LINE OVER TO STRAIGHTEN,
   AS IN 3, AND REPEAT THIS AS OFTEN AS IT IS
   NEEDED 74

9. LEADING THE FLY 82

10. THE ROD IS HELD VERY HIGH (A) SO THAT IF A FISH
    TAKES THE FLY WHEN IT HAS ARRIVED BELOW
    YOU, SLACK MAY BE GIVEN TO AVOID A BREAK,
    BY DROPPING THE ROD-POINT DOWNSTREAM AND
    TOWARDS THE BANK (B) 92

11. CAST TO 1. DO NOT ALLOW THE LINE TO GET INTO
    POSITION 2, BUT MEND IT TO 3 AND PREVENT FLY
    BEING PULLED UPSTREAM. FOLLOW LINE ROUND
    WITH ROD SO AS TO GET POSITION 4 AS SOON AS
    YOU CAN 96

12. CAST TO 1. BY THE TIME THE FLY GETS TO 3 THERE
    IS AN UPSTREAM BELLY IN THE LINE ; CORRECT
    THIS BY MENDING TO 4 AND THEN CONTINUE TO
    BRING ROD ROUND TO 5. MAINTAINING TENSION
    ON LINE WILL HELP TO KEEP THE LINE MOVING
    DOWN FASTER. 97

FIGS.   PAGE

13. CAST TO 1. NEVER LET THE LINE GET INTO POSITION
    2 AND KEEP ON MENDING IT SO THAT IT IS IN
    POSITION 3 MOST OF THE TIME. WHEN YOU GET
    TO 4 HOLD ROD AT C, AND LET THE FAST WATER
    PULL THE FLY OVER THE SLACK WATER   .   .   98

14. SHOWS HOW THE DIFFICULT AREA BEYOND A BAND
    OF QUIET WATER CAN EASILY BE COVERED. B1.
    CAST AND MEND TO B2. MEND AGAIN FROM
    3 TO 4. ALLOW FLY TO BE DRAWN GENTLY FROM
    5 TO 6 BY LETTING THE ROD SWING ROUND.
    COMPARE THE DIAGRAM WITH FIGURE 15.   .   100

15. THESE SHOW THE WAY IN WHICH A FLY CAN BE
    SUCKED DOWN BEHIND A STONE   .   .   .   101

16. HOOKING A FISH ON THE GREASED LINE. NOTE
    THAT ROD IS KEPT LOW (BOTTOM), WHILE IN TOP
    PICTURE THE ANGLER IS SHOWN WRONGLY STRIK-
    ING OVERHEAD. COMPARE THE TWO   .   .   113

17. FISHING A SUNK FLY. SHOWING METHOD OF SINKING
    FLY   152

18. FISHING SUNK FLY ACROSS A FAST RUN   .   .   154

19. FISHING EDDY BEHIND A ROCK WITH SUNK FLY
    SUBMERGED   156

20. FISHING THE EDGE OF A FAST RUN WITH SUNK FLY   157

21. CAIRNTON WATER   184

GREASED LINE FISHING

CHAPTER ONE

A. H. E. WOOD: AN APPRECIATION

By J. W. HILLS

ARTHUR WOOD was one of those remarkable men who excel at everything which they take up. He had that great executive capacity, that power of quick decision and that essential rightness which belong to men of his stamp. Though he was a business man of distinction he could undoubtedly have played a bigger part than he did in our industrial life and would have been valuable in the reorganisation that is taking place in many of our factories. In fact it is no exaggeration to say that there is no enterprise of which he was not capable. And yet he devoted much of his life to what most people regard as the trivial and the transitory or, at all events, the side issues of the world. He was a yachtsman, a gardener, a beekeeper and, above all, a fisherman, and though he came to the top, as he always would, in all four, no doubt there are those who think that his life was not fully lived because he did not try bigger things. Such men as he are blamed because they do not use their energies in doing something which the world thinks commendable. No one, it will be said, had such serviceable and adaptable abilities. Why did he not devote them to works of greater import? Certainly he lived a life most suitable for the ordinary man and most praiseworthy. He managed his Scotch estate and managed it well, he made a rock garden which people came miles to see, he shot and he fished. He lived our serene country life, which still goes on in spite of change, with his flowers, his sport, his books and his friends. All very well for most of us, it will be said; we can hardly do better. But for him, with his real executive and originating mind, with his practical imagination, his leadership, his outstanding power of seeing what ought to be done and of adapting his ideas to all the detail of action, would not he have spent his time better had he chosen some wider career?

These questions will always be asked and the answer is not always obvious. And yet I believe that men such as Arthur Wood live the most valuable and the most useful of lives. They have the courage and the sense not to do all that they might do. They choose to do what they do best; and they do it best because they love it. We are all apt to look upon the work as more important than the love of the work. And yet it is not: is any life fully lived unless the worker's heart is active as well as his brain or his hand? Not many are fortunate enough to be able to attain this. It is, of course, obvious that circumstances must be particularly favourable to them, for many of us have to do work which, if not actively distasteful, excites no pleasing emotion. But those who can attain it, gain an inner harmony and balance which gives them completeness. This is their exceeding great reward. And they are not the only gainers. They give as well as receive, and because they receive much, they give much. They are, for the rest of us, the salt and the savour of life. Without them the world would be a tasteless and a bleaker place. They are a great race, men such as Arthur Wood. They stand outside the sheep-track of the main circle. Their country is the richer for having them, and their friends the richer for having known them.

There was nothing of the eccentric or crank about Arthur Wood. No man in the world was more splendidly and gloriously normal. A magnificent body, a magnificent mind, and a will and imagination peculiarly ready for any call upon it. Nor was he only suited to carry out great works, for a friend said of him with truth that no one could deal so successfully with the ordinary emergencies of life. If the cook scalded herself, or a man had a fall out hunting, or the frost burst a pipe, or the dog bit the baby, he would know what to do ; he would take charge of the situation and everyone would recognize that he was the proper person to do so. That he did not seek notoriety was his own wish. That he did not make a mark which was obvious left him indifferent. And he had the reward which is given to men such as he : a genius for friendship and a genius for spending the best of himself on his friends.

In appearance he was tall and broad-shouldered, with exceptional depth of chest from back to front. He was obviously a man of mark and character, even at a casual view. He had rather large features, grey eyes and was clean shaved. His really immense muscular strength was not supported by strength of constitution, and for some time before his death, even when he continued fishing, he was in discomfort and often pain. I did not know him until 1927. We met as fishermen, but continued as friends. What he was in angling is told in the present book, largely in his own words, and I do not propose to repeat it.

The basis and discovery of his theory of the floating line is simple. His first step was to find out at what point in the sunk fly's course most fish take it. Secondly, how was the fly travelling at that point, that is, how did it appear to the eye of the salmon ? And, thirdly, how could he so manage rod, line and fly that wherever the fish was lying the fly should be presented in the same way ? Now all of us who were brought up in the old school know that the most deadly part of the fly's journey was when it was swinging round into the straight. That is the first answer. And if we put ourselves in the salmon's place, we shall see that the fly would then be floating down past him; not coming straight at him, which only happens at the end of its course, and not being drawn across him, as happens at the beginning, but, as it were, sidling past him and floating downstream. That is the second answer. And these two matters being determined, the practical work began, and the third answer was reached, presentation. And so clever was Arthur Wood's method that he could present his fly in this manner to a fish wherever it was stationed, whether straight below, or at an angle below, or straight across, or even across and above him. Theory and practice became one.

This was done, as the book tells, by mending the line. Now mending the line is an extremely easy phrase to use, but an extremely difficult thing to do. It required skill to invent it. And after invention it requires skill to attain it, and I believe it took Arthur Wood himself many years to become perfect. The details of method are so well described in the book that I will not repeat them. For the novice there are four points to remember. The mend is not a cast, but a lift with the arm extended and the rod held not high and not much out of the horizontal. It is made as much across stream as upstream, otherwise there is a pull on the fly. It must be made as soon as the fly lights. And it may have to be repeated two or three times in the fly's course. I should have said, by the way, that cases exist where no mend is required, where the stream runs at an evenly-increasing pace from angler to fly; but they are rare, for hardly ever can the fly be expected to fish on Wood's method all the way round without some action by the angler. To mend properly you must have a delicate touch. You must feel the line without pulling it. You must have good hands, in which Wood excelled. Very few people can make a mend right down to the knot of the line without drawing the fly, and until they do this they do not enter into the company of the great masters. The secret is to think of it never as a cast, and not even as a lift, but as a roll. Start the line downstream, and continue rolling it over, not using the point as in a cast, but merely to keep you in touch with the line. Roll it over and place, not throw it, across stream as well as up.

That is the first thing that I tried to learn, the mend. And I do not believe I have ever made a big mend, except under extraordinarily favourable conditions, which did not pull the fly slightly. But practice does much. And next I learned, and this is a first thing also, to watch the water, to bore into it so as to note all the little back-washes, eddies and strong runs which exist in a big and broken river. Here I should say that it is of immense advantage to know your river. You only do so after much labour. When you have mastered the mend you can put your fly to, and catch individual salmon rising straight opposite you in a strong and turbulent stream. And this, to quote an old writer, 'is the chiefest pleasure of angling.'

Now I will not go into the different ways of fishing different places : where the stream runs fast at your feet and slow beyond, where there is a backwater too deep to wade between you and the fast water, where rocks, with eddies below them, lie in the track of your line, or where there is a combination or permutation or variety of all these difficulties. These you will discover for yourself. But next to presentation, which ought to do the business of getting the fly into the salmon's mouth, comes your second task, which is getting the hook into the corner of his jaw. Arthur Wood once told me that though he hated being talked to whilst he was fishing, anyone could talk to him when a fish rose, meaning thereby that he liked to be distracted, since the thing to do then was to do nothing. This is not always so. For instance, in fast water if a fish takes straight below you, you must drop your hand or let out slack. But undoubtedly for the beginner it is the best advice. You avoid the dreadful mistake of raising the rod when you see the rise. You have to train yourself, or drill yourself, or kick yourself into doing the opposite. Either do nothing, or if you can reach that perfection, drop the point of the rod towards your own bank, until it nearly touches the water. Then the pull of the stream on the line will hook the fish. But habit is strong and the will

is weak, and few are the times, except when fish
are taking frequently, that I have done all this as the
book lays down. But perhaps I have learned not to
raise my hand and to drop the point. And this I
have learnt at the cost of losing many noble fish.

Such is a short summary of the Wood system.
He often told me that he liked the fly to float down
like a dead leaf. What he regarded as fatal was any
pull on it by the action of the stream on the line.
When the cast is made and mended, and the line
floating delightfully without drag, you should lead
it round by keeping the rod point in advance of it.
This is another matter of importance You must
lead the line, without pulling it, keeping just enough
touch on it to feel it, and manœuvring it so that there
is at no point what Wood called a " knuckle," that is,
a small acute curve caused by the stream. Sometimes,
when standing by me, he has called out, " You can't
get rid of that knuckle by mending ; lead the line
instead," and it will be realised that such a bend
is best put right by moving the top of the rod towards
the fisherman's bank, thereby straightening the line.
Leading is a work of handcraft and gives you a sense
of skilled control. You are always in touch with
your fly.

Arthur Wood's rods and his casts and his flies
are fully described in what follows. He turned
salmon fishing topsy-turvy. Instead of being pursued
in the cold and cloudy days of spring or autumn,

the Wood system comes to its zenith in summer, under a genial sun and a blue sky. No day could be too hot, no sun too brilliant and no water too clear and low for Arthur Wood. He did his best under conditions which, to the old angler, would have seemed hopeless.

Under conditions suiting his method, his successes were amazing. To pay for this he no doubt sacrificed something in early spring or full waters. The ghillies at Cairnton used to say : " When other rods catch fish, Mr. Wood does not."

Wood was just as happy teaching as fishing. Many and many a day when he might have got salmon he has stood by me in the water for hours together criticising each cast and going on at me until he made me do it right. These days are my most cherished memories as they are the most useful. He knew the water like a book, and wherever a fish was lying he would tell me just how the fly should be presented in order to catch it. And all the time he gave freely of his fishing knowledge, which was greater than that of any man whom I have ever met.

Never was fishing better organised than at Cairnton, more strenuous or more entrancing. Life was ordered so as to promote the catching of fish. Breakfast was at 8.30, and you had to be punctual or you heard about it ! At 9.30 you were in waders and on the way to your beat. There you fished with what success fate gave you until one o'clock, when you lunched in extraordinary comfort in one of the huts. Of these there were two, one on the upper and one on the lower water, and they really were far more than huts—they were rooms furnished with everything which the fisherman's heart could desire, with bow windows commanding the river up and down. You had luncheon with the rod with whom you shared the water, upper or lower, and after luncheon you changed beats. If it was May or early June dinner was brought out to you at half-past six and you fished on in the clear opal dusk of a northern night till half-past ten or eleven, or later. Then you staggered home, got out of your waders which you had worn for thirteen or fourteen hours, foregathered with the other rods, and talked of the day and its fortune. And usually fate decreed that some fishing mystery would be mooted. Sides would be taken, discussion raged keen, neither would yield, and perhaps it was one o'clock or more before you got to bed. But what debates we had. Great fishers gathered at Cairnton from all over the world: and with nerves on the stretch and minds alert just because our bodies were weary, we would talk that endless talk which a common pursuit provides. Those evenings dwell clearly in my mind and will always remain. And with them will remain the memory of a great and unclouded friendship.

CHAPTER TWO

TACKLE

M R. WOOD believed in the short rod for salmon fishing. This may have been due to the fact that he disliked casting with two hands. Upon one occasion he told me that he had never attempted double-handed casting, and that all his fishing, from boyhood upwards, had been carried out with short weapons.

Once he had settled down to serious salmon fishing at Cairnton he commenced a series of experiments with a view to evolving suitable rods. He soon discovered that three strengths of rod were necessary and in conjunction with the late Mr. J. J. Hardy, Managing Director of Messrs. Hardy Bros., he designed the well-known " Wood " pattern twelve-footers.

These rods were subsequently modified ; but in their original form their specifications were as follows:

No. 3, the heavy-duty rod, used for fishing the sunk fly and heavy line. Length, twelve feet. Built of " Palakona " split bamboo, with Hardy lock-fast joints, bridge rings, agate butt and end rings, rubber button. Weight, fourteen and a half ounces.

This rod fished a heavy, double-tapered line, the centre diameter of which was 16 or 16·5 Standard Wire Gauge, and it would comfortably cast any fly from a 4/0 to a 6/0½ (two-and-three-quarter inches in length).

No. 2 was also a twelve foot rod, used for heavy greased line work in Spring, and capable of standing up to the task of manhandling kelts in heavy water. Its specification was similar to the No. 1, but it was, of course, lighter all through, and weighed thirteen ounces. This rod fished a double-tapered line, the centre of which measured 17·5 or 18 S.W.G. and the line was, of course, greased when in use. This rod cast flies of from No. 1 to No. 4 sizes.

The No. 1 rod was designed for summer weather and small flies—sizes 4 to 10; weighed approximately eleven ounces, and fished a greased line with a 19 S.W.G. centre and 22 or 23 S.W.G. points.

These three rods were used for many seasons with great success; but Mr. Wood eventually made —in conjunction with Mr. L. R. Hardy—great improvements. He had fished with an American rod and being greatly struck by the balance, which was easier on the wrist than that of his own weapons, he entered into a correspondence with Mr. Hardy on the subject.

Mr. Wood was exceptionally strong in the arm and wrist and could therefore handle a very strong rod with ease—indeed he fished a sixteen-foot rod

single-handed in my presence when experimenting—
but even so, he must have found the heavy twelve
footer rather tiring to use during a long day's fishing;
and Mr. Hardy, himself no weakling in forearm and
wrist, expressed the opinion that the heavy rod was
really beyond the powers of any man—when used
single-handed.

Mr. Wood then experimented with a number of
rods in his collection and wrote to Mr. Hardy as
under :

" I have stripped the light and medium rods, that
is, I have taken off reel and rubber button; also I
have similarly stripped two other American rods and
compared. The heavy Hardy weighed 15 oz. and the
balance from the butt was at 3 ft. 8½ in. The heavy
American weighed 14½ oz. and the point of balance
from the butt was 3 ft. 3 in. The two light Hardy's
were respectively : Weight 12 oz. and 12¾ oz., and
the balances were at 3 ft. 7¾ in., and 3 ft. 8 in. The
light American weighed 14¼ oz. and the balance is
at 3 ft. ½ in. The chief point is that, taking this light
American, 14¼ oz., which is heavier than either of
your two rods yet even then feels so light in the hand
that almost all my friends can fish it single-handed,
but cannot fish with your two rods owing to the
weight being on the wrist; in the case of the American
rods the weight is right in the hand. I am anxious
to improve my rods in every possible way, and I
am sure if you could get the balance further back I

could cast six or seven yards farther than with my
present rods."

Mr. Hardy replied :

"I agree that a rod which feels light in the hand
is very probably helping you to cast farther because
the rod comes more within your power. We will
build a new rod, trying, while retaining full power,
to get the balance back into the hand as much as
possible."

Mr. Wood then said :

"Please do not make a rod $14\frac{1}{2}$ oz. just because
my other rod was that weight, but make it lighter
if you can, but if lighter, it must be in the top and not
in the butt as the balance must come back near the
hand. I find among all my friends, small or big men,
that it is not the actual weight and strength of the
rod that tires them, but the balance."

Mr. Hardy then made several rods of different
balances which Mr. Wood tried in actual fishing.
The heaviest, or No. 3, rod was an instantaneous
success ; but the No. 2, or medium rod, became the
subject of further experiments. This rod was discovered to be rather too light in the top and hence
lacking in lifting power. The No. 1 proved successful after trial.

Mr. Hardy then wrote :

"Regarding the light rod (No. 2) you will remember that you were very emphatic as to keeping
the rod light in the hand, and the only way to do

this was to make the rod with a quickish taper, butt
fairly stiff and top and middle light. If the top and
the upper part of the middle were strengthened
slightly, that would be my idea of the ideal rod."

By proceeding on these lines a new series of
12 ft. rods was evolved, which Messrs. Hardy
ultimately placed upon the market. The full specification was :

	No. 1	No. 2	No. 3
Length .	12 feet	12 feet	12 feet
Weight .	12¼ ozs.	12¾ ozs.	13½ ozs.
Rings .	Agate Butt and End, with Hardy "Full-open" Bridge Intermediate	do.	do.
Joints .	Hardy "Lockfast"	do.	do.
Sizes of line in S.W.G.	Hardy "Corona Superba" 1.B.1. Points 23 S.W.G. Centre 18 S.W.G.	Hardy No. 5 "Corona" Points 20 S.W.G. Centre 17 S.W.G.	Hardy No. 4a "Corona" Points 18½ S.W.G. Centre 16½ S.W.G.
Reels best suited for	No. 2 "St. John"	3¾" "Perfect"	4" "Perfect"

In these rods the object which Mr. Wood had
in mind, i.e., improved lightness in the hand, was
fully accomplished ; and they are, in consequence
of his interest in their design, known as the " A. H. E.
Wood " rods. As a final touch, these rods were
fitted with a new type of bridge-ring now known as
the Hardy " Full open " Bridge-ring which permitted
very easy shooting of the line, and Mr. Wood expressed great pleasure at this improvement. He
found, by actual experience, that the new rings
enabled him to shoot several extra yards of line,

thus increasing his range of action—a considerable advantage when fishing the wide pools on his water.

In consequence of these alterations the Hardy-" Wood " rods possess a peculiar action, indescribable in cold print ; but after practice, they exert a strange fascination over their owner. For the first few casts one is inclined to feel a little at sea, but once the timing has been mastered—and owing to the extra power situated near the top ferrule, the timing is certainly unusual—a vast amount of line can be thrown. The balance, also, is further back in the hand, and in consequence the rod is easier to fish with than the original models which, I frankly confess, were too much for me !

Mr. Wood also possessed a Grant Vibration Rod. These rods are, of course, spliced greenhearts. Shortly before his death, I was making a series of experiments with these and other rods, in which Mr. Wood participated. During these trials, a feature of casting, which is not so well known as it deserves to be, cropped up.

Any fly rod fitted with upright rings, bridge or snake, is subject to a serious loss of casting power at the commencement of the forward stroke. A glance at Fig. 1 will show why this occurs ; and it is particularly prevalent in the case of the very quick-action rod. As the line is lifted from the water it is under strong tension ; but as the rod comes to rest at the

Fig. I.

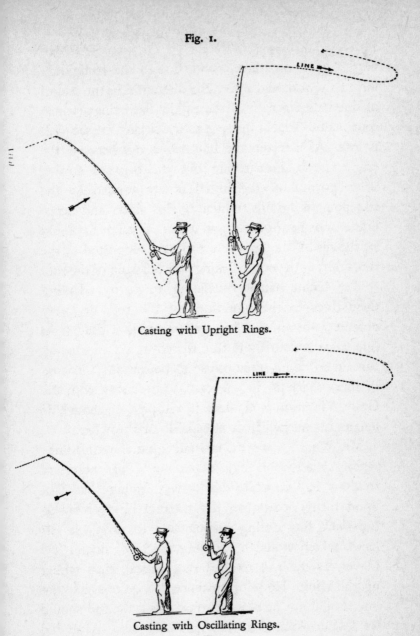

Casting with Upright Rings.

Casting with Oscillating Rings.

vertical position, the tension, due to the straightening of the rod, and hence the alteration in the length
of line between each of the rigidly fixed rings (which
cause a dead load at the spot to which they are secured)
is lost. As a result, the line bellies out between the
rings. Now, in carrying out the forward stroke,
some portion of the initial power applied by the
rod point is lost in tightening this slack, and hence
line cannot be thrown to so great a distance as would
be the case if the line were properly supported by the
rings during the entire flexing and reflexing of the rod.

The Grant patent oscillating rings, by adapting
themselves to the vibrations of the rod, do, very
definitely sustain the line, and maintain a dead tight
line from reel to fly during the entire act of casting.
But, in so doing, they refuse to permit any shooting
of line, which is, in any case, unnecessary with the
Grant Vibration Rod, since it will pick up the whole
length of line which it is capable of throwing.

Mr. Wood, however, insisted upon shooting line ;
saying that for his style of fishing it was necessary
to draw in line while the fly was fishing ; at least,
upon many occasions. His method of overcoming
the slack line during casting was to drop his left
hand, which would be holding the loose line, a few
inches, as the rod reached the vertical, thus taking
up the slack. He said, however, " I quite agree that
one should not be obliged to do this ; the rod should
be able to look after the line, and what is needed

is an oscillating ring which will both sustain the line and allow of its being shot if required. I am quite sure that the upright ring is mechanically wrong; but what is one to do when fishing the greased line? One simply must shoot the line one has pulled in."

The reader who wishes to try the Grant oscillating rings—and rods are made with both fixed (i.e. upright) and oscillating rings to choice—will find that two false casts down the side of the water will suffice to put out the loose line drawn in by hand. Personally, I have used both methods with success. I commend this interesting, and very important, little problem to the reader who is fond of experimenting.

Mr. Wood's death unfortunately cut short our correspondence on this matter, and its further history is, perhaps, beyond the scope of this volume, but so far as I am concerned the matter is still one for thought and experiment. This book is devoted to Mr. Wood and not to my own theories, which would, no doubt, appear out of place.

As a final word concerning rods, Mr. Wood remarked that many of his friends were now using strong trout rods of nine and ten feet in length, unless the water was high. He added: " I think it is quite right to use as light a rod as you care to and one that is easily handled. In the case of a big river like the Dee, there is an advantage in a twelve or fourteen foot rod. You have so many rocks to contend with on the other side of the river, and often

get a long, drowned line. Some of our pools are
over sixty yards wide, so you must have a lot of
backing, as with trout casts and a big fish you often
have to let him go where he likes, and the longer rod
is useful for holding up the line to clear rocks.
But any rod, single or double, does for this game.
Some men use a strong ten foot rod and fish it
double-handed. On the whole, I think the size of
the river and that of the fish controls the length of
rod to a certain extent."

Reels

Mr. Wood used large-diameter, narrow-drum reels
fitted with a variable check. The deep, narrow drum
enabled him rapidly to recover line when playing
a fish, without the addition of any multiplying gear,
which he did not like. One point upon which he
always insisted—and upon which any fisherman
would be wise to insist—was that the handle of the
reel should be fixed as near as possible to the peri-
phery of the drum, so giving greater leverage when
winding in against resistance.

He also was emphatic upon the need for frequent
oiling of the reel-spindle and check work. It should
be unnecessary to remind any fisherman of this, but
alas! a mere glance at the tongues, springs and
spindles of one's friends' reels shows them to be, in
nine cases out of ten, bone-dry! Personally, I believe in the use of the oil made for lubricating gun

and rifle locks; it is odourless, clean, possesses high lubricating properties, and is a great rust-preventive (steel check work rusts if aluminium does not!) Further, it does not turn sticky and clog the reel.

Lines

The lines in use at Cairnton were the ordinary double-taper, oil-dressed. Mr. Wood, in a letter to a friend, remarked that he preferred a partly-worn line to a new one, as it floated better. The reason lay in the fact that a partly worn line has a rougher surface than the new, highly polished one. This slight roughness provides a " key " for the grease, which holds better and lasts longer, in exactly the same way that the finishing coat of plaster clings to the rougher undercoat on a house wall. *Au contraire*, the brand new line has an almost slippery surface and this, combined with air and water friction, soon causes the grease to disappear. Hence the sinking of many a brand new line. Again, few lines are really pleasant to fish with until well broken-in and supple; and an old line, being flexible, gives to the eddies of the stream and is more easily manipulated when on the water.

Grease

" Hardy's Celoréne "; the special quality exported to India and other tropical climates, is the best for this work. I find that it has extra body and lasts much

longer than the usual " Celoréne " which they sell
for use at home—especially in summer. If I need
more grease on the line during the day I get my
ghillie to hold the end of the line above his head
while I walk backwards with raised rod until all the
line is run off the reel. I then shake the line very
thoroughly to make the water fly off, rub it down
with a cloth or bit of amadon, and re-grease the whole.
This I find quite effective.

Casts

Like all other very successful anglers Mr. Wood
paid great attention to the proportion of his gear;
rod, line and fly had to harmonise. When using the
strong rod with sunk line and big fly he employed
a 2/5 to 4/5 cast, according to the height of the water.
The medium rod (No. 2) fished a cast of 5/6 to 6/5,
with flies varying from No. 1 to No. 4. When the
No. 1, or light rod, was in use the casts ranged from
7/5 to 1x, according to the water; while the flies
ran from No. 4 to No. 10. These casts were parallel
and not tapered, and were knotted to the reel line
without the intervention of a twisted gut collar.

Flies

A reprint of Mr. Wood's fishing card is given
opposite; and all sizes of flies referred to in this book
are taken from it.

This card shows the sizes of some Dee hooks

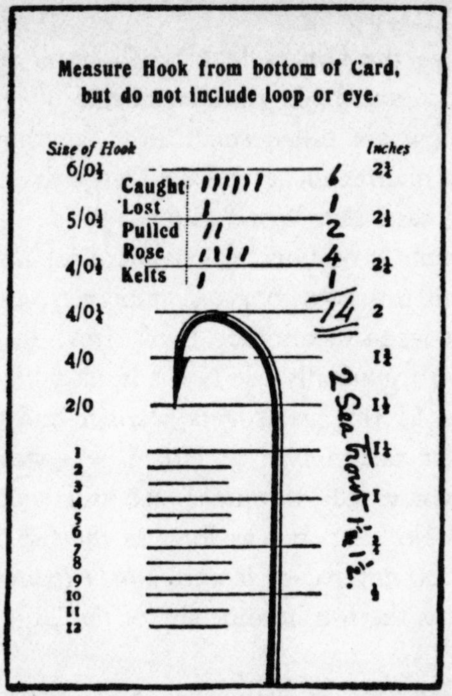
Measure Hook from bottom of Card,
but do not include loop or eye.
Size of Hook
Inches
6/0½
5/0½
4/0½
4/0½
4/0
2/0
1
2
3
4
5
6
7
8
9
10
11
12
Caught ////// 6
Lost / 1
Pulled // 2
Rose //// 4
Kelts / 1
14
2 Sea Trout 1½ & 1½.

Name AHEW CAIRNTON. Date May 5th

Pool	Weight	Fly	Size Hook	Time Landed
Cottage	7½	Blue Charm	·10	9·30 am
"	8½	"	8	9·55
"	14	"	8	10·15
"	21½	March Brown	8	10·30
Grey Mare	21½	"	10	12·40 pm
"	9¼	Blue Charm	1	7·25

39205

The Cairnton Card. Fig. 2.

which have the shanks lengthened by a quarter or
half an inch and have a moderate size of gape. No.
1 and below are called small flies; anything above
one and a quarter inches is called large fly.

Of this card Mr. Wood said:

"As there is no universal standard for hook sizes,
I made out this card to avoid ambiguity, and always
refer to it when mentioning hook sizes. In February
and March I generally use No. 1 hook with ordinary
dressing; as the water gets warmer and clearer I
use smaller sizes down to No. 6. As weather and
water become still warmer I use still smaller flies,
No. 6 to No. 12; but as long as the fish will take
a No. 6 I do not go any lower. I only reduce the size
of the fly as the fish become shy of the larger sizes of
small hooks.

"In May, and sometimes in April, these flies and
hooks are too heavy in iron and dressing for
clear water: I then use summer flies tied for
me with an extremely spare dressing, no part of it
going beyond the point of the hook. The hooks are
made of fine oval wire and have a long shank; they
swim well, and, in a stream, do not hold the water.

"Without putting any grease on the cast, enough
seems to get there to make them float, also the cast;
and in smooth water, sometimes even in strong
water, it is most difficult to keep the fly under the
surface, so that one really does want some weight
in the hook. These hooks, however, are so thin

that they cause very little drag, just enough to make them keep up near the surface when they go under ; but in actual practice, in slow running water, the fly lies on its side and floats perfectly, so the hook is evidently not *too* heavy.

" Some people have said that a fly should be opaque ; i.e., the dressing should pass no light, and that a fur body would be successful. Personally, I do not agree. I like the dressing to be as thin, transparent and misty as possible where low water flies are concerned. The older and thinner a fly becomes through wear, the better the fish seem to like it, provided the weather is hot and the water clear. I have caught fish on a practically bare hook on which there was left no body and only the head and four fibres of the wings ; also quite a number on a hook with only the body and no wing or hackle at all.

" As regards pattern, I do not believe that this matters at all. Blue Charm and Silver Blue are my stock, simply on the principle that one is more or less black and the other white and so give *me* a choice. I once fished through the whole season with a March Brown only, and got my share, and more, of the fish caught.

" Blue Charm and Silver Blue I keep in all sizes from No. 1 to No. 12, ordinary weight of hook, and March Brown, Blue Charm and Silver Blue sparely dressed on No. 4 to No. 10 light low-water irons. These last I use only in warm weather and clear water. I always start with a Blue Charm and only change it if all the sizes I try prove no good, then I try a Silver Blue. But if the water is very clear and the weather bright, I use a March Brown, and pick out the 'ripest' one in my box.

"If you rise a fish to, for example, No. 6, change to a No. 8 and you should get him, for that fish has shown you No. 6 was on the large size for that pool, place or time. If you have the right size fly on it is very rarely that you get merely a rise; the fish always means business if he comes. If, however, he rises and refuses, it is a clear sign that the fly is too big and too showy for him."

Regarding these standard patterns, Messrs. Hardy Bros. have kindly sent me the specification of the patterns approved by Mr. Wood as follows which are dressed and now sold by that firm as the " Wood Low Water Flies."

Blue Charm

Tip : Silver Wire.
Tail : G.P. Crest.
Body : Black Floss Silk.
Ribs : Silver Oval.
Hackle : Light Blue.
Wing : Mallard, Slip of Teal and Crest over.

Logie.

Tip : Silver Wire.
Tail : Crest G.P.
Body : Claret Floss Silk.

Ribs : Silver.
Hackle : Light Blue.
Wing : Under Yellow Hen Wing, Mallard over.
Cheeks : Jungle Cock.

Jockie.

Tip : Silver Wire.
Tail : G.P. Crest.
Body : Two Turns of Yellow Floss, remainder Claret.
Ribs : Silver.
Hackle : Cock-a-bondhu.
Wing : Mallard.
Cheeks : Jungle cock.

Jeannie.

Tip : Silver Wire.
Tail : G.P. Crest.
Body : Two Turns of Yellow Floss, remainder Black.
Ribs : Silver.
Hackle : Black.
Wing : Mallard.
Cheeks : Jungle Cock.

Silver Blue.

Tip : Silver Wire.
Tail : G.P. Crest.
Body : Flat Silver.
Ribs : Oval Silver.
Hackle : Light Blue.
Wing : Pintail.

Bumbee.

Tail : Tuft of Orange Wool.
Body : Two Turns of Orange Wool, remainder Black.
Ribs : Silver Oval.
Hackle : Cock-a-bondhu.
Wing : Mallard.

March Brown.

Tail : Mallard.
Body : Two Turns of Yellow Wool, remainder Hare's Ear.
Ribs : Gold Oval.
Hackle : Dark Partridge.
Wing : Hen Pheasant Tail.

Sailor.

Tip : Silver Wire.
Tail : G.P. Crest.
Body : In two halves of Yellow and Blue Seal's Fur.
Wing : Pintail Strips and Crest over.
Cheeks : Blue Kingfisher.

Green Peacock.

Tip : Silver Wire and Yellow Floss.
Tail : G.P. Crest.
Body : Blue Floss.
Ribs : Silver Oval.
Wing : Sword peacock.

Lady Caroline.

Tail : Point of G.P. Breast Feather.
Body : Reddish Brown Olive Seal's Fur.
Ribs : From different starting points Silver Flat, Gold
            and Silver Thread.
Hackle : Blue Heron.
Throat : Turn of Breast Feather of G.P.
Wing : Mallard " flat " on Body.

These flies are illustrated in the coloured frontispiece plate, q.v.

In 1932 Mr. Wood tried the " Kilroy " flies in their
original form ; and suggested to the inventor that
a series designed for use on the greased line should

be produced. Accordingly, Mr. Kilroy tied a new
type of fly and submitted it to Mr. Wood, who
wrote :

"Your flies are all right. I certainly admire the
body, or the lack of it. Most hooks are so heavily
dressed as to be useless in clear water. Your trick
of celluloid coating is a very happy idea and I should
think would glisten well. It would also certainly
stop tarnishing, I should think. You ask me to try
the experiment of putting the fly in water ; but I am
not a believer in this as water has a skin which upsets
everything below it as far as the human eye is concerned. Also, looking through a glass prevents you
seeing true detail ; but if you use a pair of water
spectacles, putting your head in the water with the
fly, you then see what the fish sees. Without them
you never really see a true object as a fish sees it.
I am afraid I am not up in optical matters, but some
of my friends are, and I have heard a good deal of
talk on the subject from them.

" The under-water glasses consist of two curved
glasses, each without power, mounted with their
convex surfaces in contact with a metal rim which
produces a water-tight chamber. When worn out
of the water there is no power in these glasses, but
under the water the curved surfaces become convex
lenses which have the effect of replacing the cornea,
so with these glasses on, and your face under water,
you get a true sight of anything you want to look at.

The trouble about looking at anything in the water through a glass-bottomed tank is that even the thickness of the glass gives you two surfaces besides the surface of the water which you see through the glass, and the angles are not always true, you only see the reflections. If you were to lie in a swimming bath with these water spectacles on and get someone to hold the fly over you, no doubt you would see what the fish see, but not so well.

" Looking through a tumbler is all right, of course, up to a point, but cannot be true owing to the glass ; you are bound to have distortion and reflection, but these would not, I conclude, upset the fish, only objects. I think a fish has extraordinarily good eyesight and sees far more than we do."

Mr. Wood also expressed the opinion that flies for greased line work should not be tied with any hard feathers. He said : " This small hook salmon fishing is done in low water and you do not want the fly to be too bunchy or create a big disturbance in the water. That is why I always had my own flies tied as flat to the hook as possible and very little of them. In summer time and when hot weather comes and sport is the best, one often has to fish in strong shallow water ; any fly that is bunchy or has stiff feathers is apt to skim on the surface or drag, and that is the reason why I personally like a bare hook or very little indeed on it, and what there is should be sitting close to the hook—just a little thin bunch like a small, thin eel. Anything bigger, even a big eye or a big head often causes a skim or wave. This sometimes attracts the fish, but more often than not he will come to the fly and stop short as it is not behaving naturally in such strong water; and that is one reason why I have a method of fishing which lets the fly float downstream and only come across the water very slowly. This stops the drag or wave, but I cannot always do it, and therefore need very thinly-dressed flies or hooks.

" I note your remarks about these delicate hooks in the hands of all anglers. Gradually fishermen are being educated to their use and are employing lighter rods with thin tops, the use of which avoids breaking these hooks in actual fishing; but where the trouble comes in is the fisherman's bad casting, touching stones and the bank behind him and not knowing the hook is broken. They always swear it broke in a fish; but that is rarely so. I seldom have one break in a fish nowadays, but I used to have plenty until I found out I was touching the bank behind me when casting, and now I have entirely cured myself."

Regarding the usual " Kilroy " greased line flies with wings and hackle, Mr. Wood made a test under fishing conditions and wrote that he and his guests had caught nine fish thereon during April, 1933.[1]

Great interest attaches to the development of Mr.

[1] A 26 lb. fish was caught on one of these flies in April, 1934.

Wood's "toys," which Mr. Kilroy tied to his specifications. These "flies" were simply the bodies of
"Kilroy" greased line flies without hackle or wings.
A head of black celluloid was placed just behind the
eye, and the bare hook was coated with transparent
celluloid to give glitter and a semi-transparent effect
after the tinsel was wound on. A small butt and very
spare tail—just a few hairs—completed the dressing.
(See Frontispiece.)

Of these "toys," Mr. Wood wrote in May, 1933:
"In past days I have fished with a bare hook, but
I like the little bit of tinsel ' gummed ' on ; it evidently
is attractive. When fishing with an almost bare hook
one is not sure if it is attractive enough. That small
bit of tinsel, without increasing the size, is just what
I want." Regarding pattern C (Frontispiece) he said,
"the new ' toy ' is just the sort of fly I like, and that
is why I keep all my old ones which get a bit thin.
I should imagine that even with strong water there
is a little life in the hairs, and the hook does not lie
still all the time, but is in motion from side to side."

In May, 1933, he wrote: " I have hardly fished at
all ; but this morning I was down for a couple of
hours and got a fish on one of your toys ; the bare
hook with the tinsel. This is the first one I have
landed ; I had a hold of two others a couple of weeks
ago, but lost them. It only shows what salmon will
take ; and I am sure these toys will be good for
sea-trout. I believe they will be very useful in hot

weather and not necessarily in shallow water ; in fact,
the fish I got was in water of from six to eight feet
deep. The two others I previously lost were in two
to three feet of water. I am going to try a bare hook
painted with coloured ' Cellire ', this will shine and
sparkle, and also give colour if wanted. It may
help to make the hook more invisible and therefore
enable one to use rather a bigger hook, which I am
always trying to do in hot weather when we have
to fish so small. I think I will get some hooks painted
for about the same length from eye towards the
bend as you cover yours with paint and tinsel. One
red, one white, one white and some other colour—
perhaps black and white rings. I believe they will be
taken quite freely."

(This, of course, is a reference to the " Redshanks "
and " Blueshanks " described in the greased line
chapter.)

Mr. Kilroy very kindly tied specimen toys for
illustration purposes, and they are shown in the
frontispiece plate.

Hooks

I expect you know how hooks are made. The
method is very nearly prehistoric and very unscientific.
I do not know when it will be altered, but making
the barb kills the metal. With regard to oval wire or
the ordinary hook flattened, I prefer the oval, for the
simple reason that I think it swims better with less

chance of the air-bubble, when fishing near the
surface, hanging on to the fly—generally on to the
bend of the hook. With the flattened hook there is
more tendency for the air-bubble to lie behind the
hook, as the flattened sides have squarer ends, leaving
a place for the bubble to cling on the hook behind.
In the case of the oval wire, the water pressure would
get round and flow easily, so keeping the bubble off.
As to strength, I think the oval-drawn wire the
stronger of the two, size for size. One edge is under
compression and the other is all the time under
tension, therefore, the flattened hook, which would
have the thicker metal, is only so much material
wasted, plus extra and unnecessary weight. I cannot
get a light enough hook for my method.

As to the question of gut attachment, after putting
on my fly or before fishing with it, I get my gut
to lie in line with the fly so that it will "stay put."
If it does not do this, I might as well give up fishing,
at least I think so ; but I have not found this trouble-
some ; at all events, with my present oval wire hooks.
I always, by the way, carry a bit of carborundum
stone to touch up a hook if it by chance has hit a
stone. Except in large-sized hooks bigger than No. 1,
I never use gut loops, but always have metal eyes.
My reason for this is that I find it far harder to change
the fly ; also the loop goes in time and you cannot
keep a stock of flies ; again, I found the loop often
affected the swim of the fly, and that is why I always

use *up-turned* metal eyes. I use a knot something like the figure eight, but not quite the same, and it is very easy to undo (Fig. 3). If the eye is on the big side, it is very easy, in tying this knot, to put it through twice, which never slips. When using fine gut I often tie it in that way.

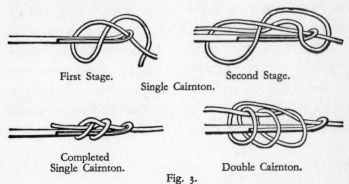

First Stage.   Second Stage.
                  Single Cairnton.

Completed
Single Cairnton.   Double Cairnton.
                       Fig. 3.

I never now use double hooks although originally I had all doubles and no singles, but it was not long before I sold the lot. Some of my letters to Crosfield (see later chapter) will explain my reasons ; he asked me to try some doubles, which I did and then wrote to him on this matter. (Mr. Wood to a friend.)

Wading Brogues

On this subject Mr. Wood wrote: " On no account have hooks and eyes, most dangerous. If you cross your feet or do anything of that sort in the water a hook may hang up in the lace of the other boot. You then find that your feet are locked together, and I have been told of a man who was nearly drowned like this. Felt soles are now becoming more common than nailed shoes. One dodge I have found useful is to have two thicknesses of felt on the soles. The first one is put on as strongly as possible and glued or cemented. The second one is also slightly cemented *and sewn*. As soon as the centre of sole and toe of the outer sole is worn through enough to just show the inner one, have it renewed. By doing this the brogue itself is never damaged. Double soles are more comfortable to walk in than singles. All brogues with felt soles should have leather and nailed heels ; and I find that the outer felt soles last me a year."

Wading Staff

" This, as perhaps you have noticed, is a very noisy affair, being metal-shod. I have got over the trouble by having an ordinary rubber cap solutioned on to the end, and with a small rivet, as the solution does not always hold well to the metal end of the stick. This rubber cap can always be bought in a walking-stick shop ; choose a good thick one. It is dead-silent in the water and does not slip ; in fact some of my friends say it is a god-send to them."

Priest

Mr. Wood invented an extremely useful little implement, which is now on the market under the title of " The Cairnton Killer." It is made of rustless steel, and is of convenient size to slip into a pocket, while the head is heavy enough to despatch any salmon. This priest is, I think, one of the neatest and most efficient patterns now obtainable.

Gaffs

Mr. Wood believed in solid wood handles for gaffs. He said: " Those Malacca cane and even other cane gaffs are always dangerous things ; they go with soft rot, especially when they occasionally get wet. I would not own such a thing as I have seen so much trouble with them. On many occasions I have known them break and leave the gaff-hook in the fish, which got away. I expect he would soon get rid of the gaff and have a quiet laugh to himself. Unless you get the gaff through a blood-vessel or the wind bag, the fish, as a rule, seem to get over it pretty easily."

CHAPTER THREE

MR. WOOD'S CASTING METHODS

AS a single-handed caster, Mr. Wood ranked very high. Using the twelve-foot rods previously described, his normal fishing cast was from twenty-five to twenty-eight yards; but on occasion he would cast up to thirty-five yards. Personally, although I watched his casting with admiration, I always felt that his great skill became more apparent after the line was on the water; in the matter of controlling a drifting line he stood absolutely alone. A few other men—as tournament records show—may have thrown a longer line; but I have never seen his equal in watermanship. If there is a better waterman alive to-day, he must be extraordinary—a superman, in fact!

Mr. Wood was very modest concerning his casting abilities; all he would say was: " Living on the water for four months of the year (February, March, April and May) as I do, I ought to be able to cast."

He was very particular as to the balance of his rods, and kept a number of weighted rod-buttons with which he experimented until a comfortable balance had been obtained; and he preferred to

grip his rod rather high up—close to the top of the
cork handle. All short and moderate-length casts
were made with the arm slightly bent, as shown in
Figure 4.

The stance he adopted was the now well-known
half-sideways position; left shoulder and leg advanced

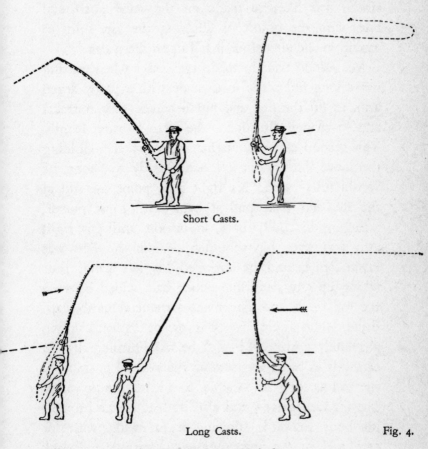

Short Casts.

Long Casts.   Fig. 4.

Mr. Wood's Casting Methods.

towards the point to which he desired to cast. The rod was then raised and pulled back across the chest, with an easy movement, the hand travelling in an almost horizontal plane until the rod reached the right shoulder, where it remained steady until the line was fully extended in the air. The forward stroke was likewise made on the same horizontal line, with the object of allowing the line fully to extend in the air before it fell upon the water.

Mr. Wood usually made two casts when putting out a long line; the first, made with a partly-flexed arm, to lift the line and put it square across stream and so change direction; the second to get length. This second cast was fascinating to watch. Holding the loose line in his left hand, ready to shoot, he would fully extend his right arm, point the rod at the fly, and then pull it back with great power, swinging his body back in unison until his right arm was over his shoulder. While the line was extending behind he dropped his left hand, thus taking up any slack line which had bellied between the rod rings, and then made a tremendous forward drive. The right arm was swept forward in an absolutely horizontal plane, the wrist turning slightly upwards in order to maintain the vertical position of the rod as long as possible, to add to the power of this forward drive—and also its length—he brought his body forward, allowing it to swing with his arm, and, at the proper moment, released the slack line in his left hand. The result was one of the most astonishing exhibitions of shooting a line that I have ever seen; I would not care to estimate the number of yards which he habitually shot, but of this I feel sure, that few, if any, fishermen have equalled Mr. Wood in this part of the fly-caster's technique.

The secret probably lay in a combination of three factors: First, the elimination of all slack line at the commencement of the forward stroke; Second, the very long and powerful forward drive; and Thirdly, in very correct timing.

The heavy rod, used when fishing a sunk line, was very powerful, and yet, when its owner was casting a long line single-handed, I have seen it bend like a trout rod under the backward lift! Mr. Wood used to say: "Of course, I happen to be geared strong enough for it; but perhaps it does require a bit of brute force to make it work!"

The back-lift of the long cast is worth the attention of the beginner. It will be noticed the hand is travelling backwards upon a slightly rising course, the object of this procedure is to allow the line time properly to extend in the air before it has fallen below the true horizontal plane. In order to obtain a really good cast two things are essential: that the line is fully extended prior to the commencement of the forward stroke; and that the line, when coming forward, should have as narrow a curve of entry as possible—in other words, the line should form more or less of a right angle with the rod when the latter is just about to commence the forward stroke. As the rod goes forward, the more its tip follows the horizontal the narrower will be the line's curve of entry. This was Mr. Wood's method; his long forward stroke, made in an almost horizontal plane, provided not only a narrow curve of entry, but very great power; and in consequence his line possessed sufficient momentum to draw out a great length of slack line when the time came to shoot.

He was very emphatic upon the necessity, when using upright rings, of taking in the slack which appeared when the rod straightened after the back-lift. As he said: " The forward stroke is not very long at the best, and it is important to use every inch of it if you are putting out a long line; there-fore, if you waste any of the stroke in taking up slack line you lose power and consequently distance."

Again, he was of the opinion that many anglers are afraid to bend their rods for fear of breaking them; in many cases they do not use the full power of the rod. I am not to be taken as stating that he advocated brute force; but he did believe in making the rod work for its living.

The other great point which he made when dis-cussing casting was the carelessness of the majority of fishermen. His view was that, except in the case of a few enthusiasts, the vast majority of fishermen took little or no trouble with their casting; and that, if they were casting badly, they would not take the trouble to think out the cause.

Throwing a slack line is sometimes difficult; the angler who has learned to throw a straight, tight line occasionally finds difficulty in deliberately placing it in festoons upon the surface. Mr. Wood's methods varied according to whether he wished to place slack line near the fly or farther back. In the latter case, he would make an ordinary forward cast and, as the line straightened out, would wave the rod-point in a serpentine path, but in a horizontal plane. The effect of this manœuvre was that the front portion of the line, having originally received a straight impetus, would extend in a direct line upon the water; while the part nearer the rod would fall in serpentine curves. This cast is comparatively easy to execute; but the successful placing of slack close to the fly is not quite so simple.

Mr. Wood used two methods in my presence. The first consisted of premature shooting of the loose line.

Mr. La Branche, in his chapter in the *Lonsdale Library* volume on *Salmon*, has aptly described this process as " deliberately losing control of the fly." In other words, the experienced angler has to do exactly what the beginner does willy-nilly; shoot his line at the wrong time. This is remarkably difficult; one's instinct is to let go at the usual moment, and it requires a distinct effort of will to overcome the more or less mechanical habit of releasing line at the correct instant. The timing is rather a nice matter; too early means that the whole line falls in a mess; too late results in too straight a line, since one is releasing at practically the correct moment for throwing an orthodox line. Properly hit off, however, the line falls in a very satisfactory state, all the slack being near the fly.

The other method, that of checking the rod, when the line is practically straight in the air, is not so easy to accomplish with a long line. Mr. Wood, however, used to cast a long line and then, just before the fly alighted, pull back the rod-point. The line and cast fall in a slack curve, or curves—usually a reverse curve like an S—while the bulk of the line remains more or less straight.

It was not often that he threw a dead-straight line in actual fishing, usually he required a little slack in one part or the other; in fact, he said to me: "Do not throw too tight a line, give yourself a foot or two of slack to play with; it is so helpful when you are lifting the line to mend the cast"; of which, more anon.

If I may be allowed to quote my own experience, I would say that, after many seasons spent in endeavouring to throw as straight a line as possible, and feeling elated when I did so, I found the effort of will-power—or memory, call it what you will—necessary to prevent one doing so unconsciously a distinct trial. Indeed, to the sunk-fly fisherman of some seasons' experience the mastering of the greased-line technique calls for constant self-control until the new habits are acquired.

To the sunk-fly fisherman, the whole business is topsy-turvy; almost crazy. The straight, tight line is unnecessary; the mending is a new and hitherto unpractised feature; leading the line with the rod instead of holding the point back; dropping the rod when a fish comes to the fly; allowing the current to strike your fish for you—here is enough to make the sunk-fly man doubt his own sanity! But once old habits have been jettisoned (and they are apt to cling like the ivy) the fisherman finds himself in a new world, in which, as he advances, all kinds of new and undreamed-of possibilities appear. Salmon are hooked in parts of the water hitherto unfished; they are caught on days previously dismissed as hopeless; hot sun and clear water are welcomed instead of being condemned, and the fishing season is often prolonged far beyond the date normally regarded as the limit of the Spring sport.

And that is not all. The greased line method infallibly teaches the least observant angler many things of which he was hitherto entirely ignorant. He will learn more about salmon and their way of taking a fly; more of the way of a fly in a stream; more, in short, of the art of salmon fishing in one season than ever he had dreamed of. This is no exaggeration. Mr. Chaytor has said that the percentage of skilful fishermen is greater among trout anglers than salmon fishers—Why? Because the former, from sheer necessity, have been compelled to study the currents and their effect on line and fly, since a dragging fly is utterly useless. No trout in full possession of his senses would take a dry fly which behaved in an unnatural manner; and certainly a hardened old veteran of the chalk streams would retire into cover, probably making some rude remark about novices to himself!

On the other hand, the sunk-fly salmon fisher cannot see how his line and fly are behaving; they are well below the surface. Again, apart from the select company of experts—such men as Messrs. Crosfield, Pashley, Traherne and Kelson—many of us were inclined to follow the advice of our ghillies without troubling to think for ourselves. In my own case, I found that I had become a sort of automaton, mechanically casting always at the same angle.

Enter Mr. Wood; and *nous avons changé tout cela!* To my mind, it is impossible to estimate the changes which his method will bring about. Already the tide is strongly flowing; converts are daily being made and, when these proselytes are in their turn, " rated A.B.," they will, no doubt, add their quota to our store of knowledge, and thus shall the sport be benefited. Of one thing I am sure; this method provides more opportunities for the study and observation of salmon and the problem of catching them than any other known to man.

Plates 2—3

Top : A. H. E. WOOD PLAYING A FISH.
NOTE THE SIDE STRAIN.

Bottom : THE SALT VATS.

Plates 4—5

Top : A FISH JUST HOOKED.
NOTICE THE JETTY BARELY COVERED BY WATER.

Bottom : KELPIE.

CHAPTER FOUR

GREASED LINE FISHING

I

FIRST PRINCIPLES

WHAT is greased line fishing ? It is a method of angling which presents the fly in an entirely natural manner, and which ensures that the fish, having taken the fly, is soundly hooked. Further, it is a method which enables the angler to attack a particular fish, as does the chalk stream dry-fly fisherman ; to observe the entire process of rising and hooking ; to fish with light tackle ; to learn, consciously or unconsciously, the art of watermanship—the mere watching of a floating line inevitably compels the least-observant fisherman to study the behaviour of the currents—and finally it is applicable to almost any condition of water and weather.

The basic idea is to use the line as a float for, and controlling agent of, the fly ; to suspend the fly just beneath the surface of the water, and to control its path in such a way that it swims diagonally down and across the stream, entirely free from the slightest pull on the line. This idea, is, of course, entirely opposed to that of the normal sunk fly procedure. For purposes of comparison, the following tabulation will be found useful :

SUNK FLY

(1) The fly travels at mid-water depth.

(2) The fly, being held by a taut line, travels far more across stream than down ; and presents a tail-end view to the fish.

(3) The fly is rigidly held against the current by a taut line, hence the only life shown by the fly is the play of wings and hackle caused by the action of the current, in addition to any jerking motion imparted by the rod top or by handling the line.

(4) The fly is being held against the stream both before and after the instant at which the fish takes it.

(5) The fish is taking a fly which is, at all times, being held back from him ; i.e., he is taking against the line tension, and feels an unnatural resistance.

(6) The line being taut, there is an instantaneous pull on the fly, tending to draw it out of the fish's mouth before it has closed.

(7) The angler has no choice as to where and when he may hook the fish : the line being tight and leading upstream, pressure is automatically applied (unless the angler sees the fish come to the fly, which cannot always be the case when the fly is sunk) and the hook either comes out or takes hold.

(8) The line, being sunk, is very largely out of control.

GREASED LINE

(1) The fly travels just, and only just, submerged.

(2) The fly travels more down than across, due to being fished on a more or less slack line ; and presents a side view to the fish, i.e., the whole of the fly is visible, not merely the tail end.

(3) The fly, being fished in such a way that it is entirely free from line-pull, swims in a natural manner; wobbling, swimming, rising and falling with the play of the eddies exactly as would an insect, or little fish which was in trouble. The very light feathers work with the action of the water, and the *whole* fly is visible to the fish.

(4) The fly is going with the stream, and with no weight behind it, at all times.

(5) The fly floats naturally straight into the salmon's mouth, and the stream's tendency is to push the fly farther back towards the throat. There is no tension, no resistance, everything is easy and natural.

(6) The line being slack, there is ample time for a fish to take, and, if he wishes, to chew the light fly.

(7) The angler always sees his rises, and gives slack. This slack line is swept downstream by the current, and, in so doing, draws the hook into the back corner of the fish's mouth. It is always possible, therefore, for an expert angler to hook his fish in the part of the mouth which offers the most secure hold.

(8) The floating line is at all times —unless grievous errors are committed—*completely* under control.

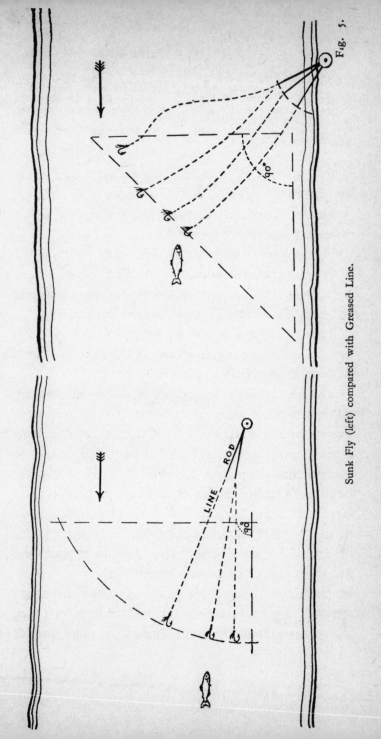

Sunk Fly (left) compared with Greased Line.

Fig. 5.

SUNK FLY	GREASED LINE
(9) In certain situations only a limited portion of the actual holding water can be fished, even if it is within casting distance.	(9) All the holding water within casting distance can be fished in a proper manner, and drag eliminated.
(10) Drag is the bugbear of the sunk-fly fishermen.	(10) Drag can be completely eliminated.

It will be seen that the greased line completely and entirely revolutionizes the practice of fly fishing ; in the words of Mr. Eric Taverner: " A new world is spread before one's eyes."

Figure 5 shows the main differences between the old and the new methods, and, studied in conjunction with the table of comparisons, should serve to elucidate the basic differences between greased line and sunk fly.

The entire process of rising and hooking a fish can be followed by a study of Figure 6—drawn under the supervision of Mr. Wood.

The line at A, having been cast across and slightly downstream, is drifting towards the fish, and, as shown by the dotted line and arrows, he comes to meet it. Notice that the line A is very slightly curved downstream. A glance will show that this curvature helps to present the fly broadside-on to the fish ; but it must not be allowed to develop into drag— of which, more anon. In this instance the fish missed, or could not quite make up his mind to take the fly, so he swam round in the circular course shown by the drawing until his head was once more upstream. By this time the fly had drifted on to B, where once again the fish missed it. The angler,

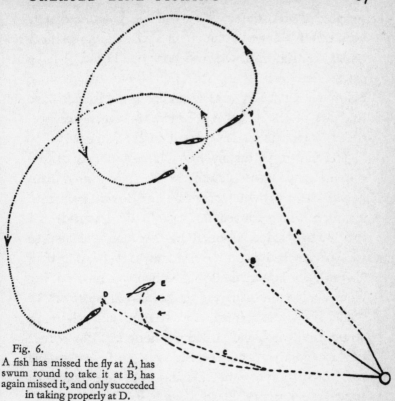

Fig. 6.
A fish has missed the fly at A, has swum round to take it at B, has again missed it, and only succeeded in taking properly at D.

however, allowed the fly to continue on its way, moving his rod downstream as shown. Again the fish completed his circle, and, at D, he decided to take the fly. Mr. Wood has said: " When a salmon goes for the fly more than once in the same cast, it swims in a kind of loop downstream and comes round to take the fly broadside-on, and does the same again and again if necessary. All this takes place just under the

surface of the water. You can see it all, and it is
very trying to the nerves ; but you must keep them
under control, until the iron has gone home. I have
often seen fish going through these manœuvres,
before taking the fly, and a number of my friends have
told me of the same experience. In every instance,
the fish appears to have acted in the same way."

The fish took the fly into his mouth and drifted
on, up- and across-stream, to E. Note what happened. The current forced the line downstream into
a curve, which caused the cast to lie alongside the
fish. The angler dropped his rod-point almost to
the surface and parallel with the bank, thus giving
all the slack line he could. The line was now pulling
from behind the fish, and as he moved upstream to
make his escape from this strange and alarming
strain, tightened, and pulled the hook into the corner
of his mouth. The current was thus responsible
for hooking the fish. During the time taken to
travel the distance D to E, the fish was probably
chewing the fly ; and as the hook was so light and
thin, he did not at once spit it out. By the time he
reached E, however, the line had begun to drag, and
the fly was drawn into the corner of the mouth,
which is quite the toughest part thereof. Notice also
that, until the line bellied, the fly had no pull upon
it ; it was quite free and unattached, so to speak ;
everything *felt* perfectly natural to the fish, and no
doubt he imagined that he had scored a point in at

last annexing this attractive little morsel which he
had so persistently chased!

That is the story of a perfect presentation, the ideal
at which the beginner should aim; and it serves to
illustrate the principles of the greased line method.
Before entering into the details of the craft, a short
account of its origin, in the actual words of the
inventor, is plainly due.

II

THE BIRTH OF THE IDEA

One afternoon in July, 1903, I was fishing an
Irish river. The weather for some time past had
been exceptionally hot and dry, so that the river had
dropped considerably and was very clear. I had
had no sport all day and sat down to think beside
a pool full of salmon that had steadily refused to
look at a series of flies, presented to them, as I thought,
in every possible way. Shortly afterwards, I saw
one fish and then another rise to something floating
down on the surface of the water. This continued
at irregular intervals, and at length I was fortunately
able to observe the cause; namely, a sort of white
moth similar to those often seen amongst the heather.

I went to the head of the pool, which consisted
of an eel-weir, and there found a number of salmon
lying with their noses pushed right up to the sill.
As luck had it, I happened to have with me a white
Moth trout fly; this I tied on the cast and sat on the

plank-bridge over the weir. Then, holding the gut
in my hand, I dibbed the fly over them. After some
minutes, one of the salmon became curious enough
to rise up to examine the fly, but at the last moment
thought better of it; this I believe was due to its
attention having been distracted by my feet, which
were dangling over the plank, barely six feet away
from the water. I changed my position, knelt on
the bridge and let down the fly. This time the
fish came more boldly at the fly and it was followed
by others; but I had pricked several before I realised
that, because I was kneeling directly above them,
I was, in striking, pulling the hook straight out
of their mouths. So I changed my tactics, and, by
letting go the cast at the right moment, succeeded
in dropping the fly actually into the open mouth
of the next fish that came to it. I then picked up
my rod, ran off the bridge, and made all haste downstream. All this time the line and cast were slack
and floating down; yet when I tightened on the
fish, I found it had hooked itself. By the use of
this trick I landed six fish, lost others and pricked
more than I care to say, all in a few hours. After that
experience, I discovered myself fishing on the surface
or as near it as I was able. The final advance came, when
I started using a greased line to assist in keeping the fly
in the right position, and I thus evolved out of a simple
experiment what has become a most interesting mode
of salmon angling, the greased line method.

I found with practice that one could hook a fish where one liked; that is, place the hook by manipulating the line to the position one wished in the fish's mouth. This sounds a tall order, but is not so difficult as it seems. I have often told friends who were watching me fish that I was willing to bet that, having hooked the fish, the hold would be in the corner of the mouth. At a shilling a time I have done quite well out of it!

When I was developing this system, I had over forty fish come at me in a day and only landed fourteen, if I remember right. The majority of the others were pricked. This sort of thing happened so often that I set to work to try and control the hooking of fish. I still have a lot to learn, but am steadily reducing the number of pulls. This is entirely due to the position of the line on the water.

Further, my experience of greased line fishing has shown me that a salmon is more ready to take a fly on or just beneath the surface than at any other level, except very near to the bottom. I therefore aim at keeping the fly at the surface, or sink it right down to the stones; and I have entirely forsaken the ordinary practice, which causes the fly to swim in mid-water.

Double or False Casting & Lifting Line Over

If I am fishing in warm weather, I usually make a double or false cast every time, as it is not easy to lift a long line from its position downstream and all at one cast place it upstream and across, if there is a high bank behind. By pulling in some yards of line, then lifting and making a short false cast square across, it becomes easy to lift the shortened line high behind and to shoot a great length of it upstream and across. By this means also I am very much more accurate in placing the fly where I want, and can be sure of placing it lightly enough to float

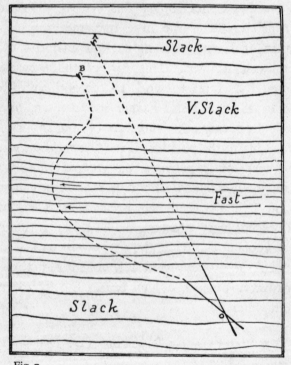

Fig 7.
The result of Casting across a fast current into an area of slower water and leaving the line to look after itself.

on the surface. When making a cast to this or any other place, do not aim the fly at a spot in the water, unless a gale is on, but try to place it a foot or two in the air, over the spot where you want it to fall, and let the line drop lightly on to the water.

Even in February, except in flood water, I do most of my fishing with a greased line and a No. 1 Blue Charm. In broken water I cast rather more upstream than the orthodox cast of a salmon fisherman, then lift my line off the water and, without moving the fly, turn over a loop of line upstream and *across* to prevent any drag on the fly.

The lifting over of a line is done to correct a fault, namely, to take the downstream belly out of a line and thus relieve the pull or pressure of the current on the line, which is communicated to the fly and exhibits itself as drag (Fig. 7). But if the line is proceeding at an even pace and shows no sign of going to drag, there is no need to mend the cast. On the other hand, if the current continues to belly the line, but before it gets a drag, lift again and continue to do so as often as you can see a drag forming (Fig. 8).

Do not on any account acquire the *habit of mechanically lifting over*, no matter how the current runs. Always have some reason for doing it : to prevent drag or, more often, to control the speed at which the fly crosses the river.

This mending or lifting over is effected by the raising of the elbow and by a turn of the wrist,

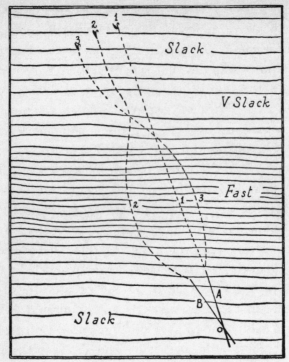

Fig. 8.
Cast to 1. The current acts on the line and 2 is formed.
Lift line over to straighten, as in 3, and repeat this as
often as it is needed.

which makes the rod follow evenly a semicircular
path, point and butt moving in unison. It is a lift,
not a back cast, and in direction should be across
stream as well as up. The line should be removed
from the surface of the water by raising the rod
almost horizontally and keeping the arm stiff, that is,
the point of the rod should usually be no higher than
the butt. It should then be swung right or left

with a *gentle* circular sweeping movement and put down where desired. If there is much rough water or a strong stream, it is useful to start lifting the line by a slight movement of the rod downstream, this prevents drag or friction, which would move the fly, and the line comes off the water more cleanly. If the water you are fishing is fast enough to need it, the first lifting of the line should be made immediately the fly has settled and without losing the fraction of a second. At first you will find that, in doing this, you will pull your fly through the water, but with practice you will soon be able to lift a long line right down to the cast without disturbing the fly. And even if you do pull it, the effect will only be felt while it is travelling a foot or so, and it will then begin to fish properly. Whenever you feel the pull of the line on the rod, you know that drag has been set up; something is wrong and needs correcting, because drag prevents the fly from fishing in such a way that a salmon can take it without *coming short*.

Further advice on mending is contained in the following letter from Mr. Wood:

That mending business I find very hard to describe, yet I have shown hundreds how to do it. They come on Sundays for tea at Cairnton and I give them a lesson if they ask for it, and this mending is the chief thing they have any trouble with. They flick and jerk the rod about anywhere. My trouble is I do it unconsciously, of course sometimes moving the fly if I am careless, and sometimes if I am not, as of course there are places where one gets the line held by the eddies; but even if the fly does jump a bit it will do no real harm.

Having made the cast and got a belly in the line, my hand and rod are close in front of my body in lifting, the point of the rod may be one foot or four feet from the water, it does not matter much, but it should *not be held high up*. I then lift the point of the rod with a stiff arm downstream and up (into the air) to clear it off the water without friction, then, continuing the swing *upstream* I keep the arm more or less stiff—after raising it from the shoulder in a horizontal position, simultaneously straightening the arm. This throws a slackness in the line between you and the fly.

Perhaps a few remarks which the fishermen make when they come here may help you:

" I did not know it was so easy as that."

" I always jerked it much too quickly."

" I did not lift with the water and did it much too quickly. You seem to do it so very slowly and quietly."

Always mend to some particular spot down the line, that is, don't lift the whole line unless you have to, only down to the eddy or whatever it is that is causing the drag. The first thing to master is lifting without really dragging the fly any great distance; once you get that right I think you will find the rest comes easy. Do not throw too tight a line when you cast, if the water is strong; give yourself a foot or two of slack so as to be able to lift inwards before the point of the rod goes outwards and round. Finally, if the rod bends while you are mending, it means that you are using too much force, the whole thing is quite *gentle* and *slow*.

In some kinds of water, particularly where the speed increases evenly from where you are standing to where the fly falls, you need not mend the line at all. You will find that the fly fishes for itself, provided you are casting downstream as well as across. But you should never cease watching your line. On the other hand, in very quick or broken water, you may have to mend twice, or even three times, as the fly comes round. All this you will discover for yourself by practice and, if you are like· me, you will also find that you have added a fascinating series of experiments to the pleasure of fishing and will get fish, when anglers using the old methods do not.

By mending the cast, I am able to check the speed of the fly all the way across and to bring it round as slowly or as quickly as I like, close to the bank or into dead water near the shore. The slower the fly travels in cold water (33° F. to 50° F.) the more chance there is of getting the fish to come out of the deeps ; and the same is often true of shallow pools. But when the water is warmer, the question of the speed of the fly is not important ; even then I rarely fish a fly fast. In February and March when the water is cold, fish are generally to be found in the dead, deep waters or in slowly-moving streams. If in these places the fly hardly moves and begins to sink, draw in line with your fingers very slowly and keep the fly as near the surface as you can, but do not be in any hurry.

At any time when you see that the fly is going to drag or the line is getting below the fly, lift your line off the water to a point beyond where the drag starts and place it again upstream of the fly. With practice this can easily be accomplished by the circular sweep of the rod as previously described. In fact, the line can at any time be lifted, unless it is held by an eddy you should have noticed beforehand and have made allowances for, by placing it upstream or downstream and thus controlling the speed and position of the fly.

When I am using the light rod and finest tackle, I often cast rather more upstream and across, as in dry fly fishing, and let the fly and line float and drift down with the current. If the fly floats and skims when the line is fully extended down (and across) the pool, straighten the line on the surface and give it a sharp jerk, which should put the fly under; then fish it round to the bank at any speed you like. A jerk on the line, before the line is straight, will make it sink in the nearest eddy and have no effect on the fly. In this way the advantages of dry fly and wet fly are combined, for in the early stages the fly fishes dry and finishes up sunk, just below the surface.

Greasing the Line

It is best to grease the line thoroughly before starting every morning. If it is for the first time, rub the grease well in, and do not hurry over the job; do it thoroughly. Occasionally I treat the whole line; but every morning I make a point of greasing about thirty-five yards. Rub it well in, do not leave more surplus than you can help to come off on to your rod or hands and, as far as possible, keep the rod rings free from grease. After the first application, do not again grease the last yard or so next to the cast, as so much gets on to this bit in actual work; but if you find the knot attachment to the cast sinking, you should give the last yard some grease, but *never* grease the cast. In cold weather, one application of grease should easily last the day; but, in summer or hot weather, it is often necessary to grease the line again, at lunch and tea-time, or whenever you find it does not float easily in quiet water.

In slow-running water there is little difficulty in keeping the line afloat. The trouble is that grease soon gets on the gut, which then floats, and so does the fly. If you want the fly to sink, a sharp jerk will generally pull it under. If this does not succeed, rub lightly the cast and last yard of line with a bunch of dead grass; this usually cures the trouble.

In strong, oily water you will not find much trouble, but watch carefully for a sucking eddy or swirl and prevent the line getting into it, by lifting either up or downstream, whichever suits you; otherwise you will get a drowned line and lose control.

In strong, broken water make your cast nearly square across, then, before the line becomes tightly held by the eddies, lift it upstream, without moving the fly. When you see all is right with the fly, lead the line downstream, just holding it with the point of the rod enough to prevent it going as fast as the current, without actually drowning it.

Leading the Fly

A word about this " leading " the fly. I find in practice that it is a great point to lead the line with the rod as so. as you can and not follow it. By moving the rod in advance of the line—but not of course dragging it—you help the fly to swim more downstream than across. This dropping downstream is extremely valuable, and whenever you can do so you should allow the fly to drop as much downstream as you possibly can. Suppose you stood in the middle of a clock face and cast to 12 o'clock. Throw a *slack* line and hold the point of the rod up after the fly has dropped on the water at 12 o'clock. By the time it has drifted to 11 o'clock the fly is still almost straight downstream from 12 o'clock instead of following the rim of the clock face in a circle. By 10 o'clock the fly is actually outside the clock face, and began to be so at 11 o'clock, finally ending up well outside the circle at 9 o'clock. Actually, while leading, the point of the rod is raised into the air. This lead in the air gives a belly in the line which enables the fish to take the fly upstream without getting an immediate pull from the rod. I generally throw a slack line which gives me as much dropping downstream of the fly as possible. See Figure 9.

There is a tremendous lot in this leading; it serves several useful purposes. If the rod were held steady, the fly would come round in more or less a true circle; but when leading, the rod-point is going downstream in advance of the line, leading and coaxing it down as well as across. This leading has another advantage; the rod is in the position it should be when you tighten the line on a fish, that is, in towards the bank and not up into the air—a *fatal* mistake that lifting into the air—as when leading it comes more natural to continue the stroke in towards the bank; besides the advantage of letting the fly go farther downstream, a much flatter curve than the true circle.

As soon as the fly gets round to your side, it may pay you to keep the rod-point *behind* the line instead of in front of it and gradually raise the point; this prevents a sudden snatch that sometimes occurs when a fish lying below you takes the fly when the line is taut. Always allow for a certain slackness in the line out of the water, and be on your guard against any drag or the drowning of any part of it. It does not matter how slack the line is, so

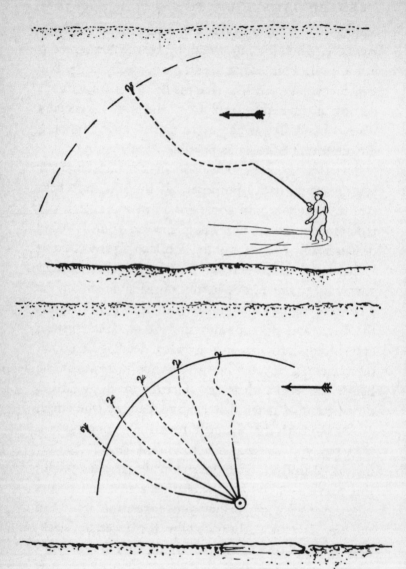

Fig. 9.

Leading the Fly. Note raised rod-top.

long as the fly is fishing as you want it, for you can always ensure enough movement in the fly by giving a free hand to the surface eddies and by letting the line guide the fly where it wants to go.

I should like to say again how very important this leading is, because whenever you can do it— and of course in some water you cannot—invariably the hook has a firm hold in the back of the fish's mouth. You can hardly help hooking it there!

I like to have a *very* slight downstream curve in the line (Fig. 9) as it drifts down, so that the fish can see the whole of the fly; and by leading and, of course, mending upstream if the curve becomes too pronounced, I often succeed in doing so. Try to get this curve if you can, but never allow the slightest drag.

Presentation

I find the best angle at which to present the fly is that which shows it broadside on to the fish; the latter invariably comes some yards to meet the fly, which is taken by it across its mouth. This is the ideal and in straight-forward fishing usually happens; the result is that, as the fish is travelling upstream and across, it takes the fly with it and in consequence the line is bellied downstream and the cast pulls the fly across into the angle of the jaw. You will find the point of the hook has gone well home and that there has been no need to strike. *Wait till you see the line being held or pulled on the surface of the water* and then tighten by moving the rod in towards your own bank, but do not on any account strike. *Do not lift the point of the rod*, but keep the line on the water all the time and move the point of the rod towards your bank at whatever level it was when the fish took. In other words, continue fishing as if nothing had occurred and no salmon were after the fly.

There are, of course, all sorts of eddies and places where the fish lie, and all have to be fished differently, so as to present the fly to the fish at the angle at which it is best able to see, most likely to be tempted and not come short. Avoid any unnatural drag at all costs. As there is little a fish does not see, the fly ought to behave naturally all the time, as an insect or other live creature would do in the water, and try to let the fly move with all the eddies it meets, as will any living thing that is trying to move in the water with the stream and across. If you swim across a river, you have to swim at an angle to the stream and make use of all the eddies ; but if you had a thick rope tied to your waist which some-one on shore was holding, you would soon be in trouble. The current would get hold of the rope and belly it downstream, then you would have to struggle hard and face more upstream, and in the end get pulled down backwards. No living creature behaves in that way, and the fish will wonder what a dragging fly is, and, even if they go for it, it will probably be dragged out of their mouths—" fish coming short," so called !

The greased line, if fished properly (and this is by no means the case every time), has no drag and often is all slack and crooked ; but, nevertheless, you are controlling the speed of the fly and the angle at which it crosses the stream. Unless you have lost control of the line, you can at any time lift the line off the water and place it where it should be ; you can then put the fly where you want and make it swim properly.

When you are wading down a long pool or are in strong water, take up your position and start with a short line. Continue to pull off a yard or so at every throw, until you have drawn off all the line you can comfortably cast. Reel up more than half of the line and then move to a fresh position about half way down what you have already covered, start again with a reasonably short line and progressively cast as far as you can. The advantages of this method are manifold. It is so much easier, when you are wading in strong water, than is taking a step or so between each cast, and the fly is shown to the salmon at different angles ; you can fish more accurately and with less trouble ; and it is more interesting than the " step and cast " method.

In the case of a pool having a jetty at the head —as some of mine have—you can stand on that jetty, cast as far as you can and then let out another yard of line ; and doing this each cast, so you can fish forty yards or so without any trouble—just

letting it drift down, and this I find most paying
in hot weather.

Hooking

When using fine tackle, take great care the rod,
line, cast and fly shall all balance and work together
for accurate and long casting. Naturally, these
small flies and hooks do not hold all the fish you
hook ; indeed, it is surprising that with such small
hooks it is possible to land salmon at all. However,
as the fish takes the fly on the surface, you can see
exactly the manner of its taking, and that is a great
help in learning how to hook a fish. You can almost
always hook a fish where you like by controlling
your nerves and the fly. For instance, when you are
fishing a streamy bit of water and a fish takes the
fly, you will, if you move or strike at once, most
likely pull its nose ; but if you wait until it goes
down (and even a little longer), you will find every
time you have hooked the fish in the angle of the jaw.

With a No. 1 hook down to say, size 4, it is
necessary to tighten *fairly* quickly *when* you feel the
fish ; or if your line is slack, when you see that the
part of line nearest the fish begins to move. The
reason of this is that the fish feels the hard iron of
the larger fly and rejects it. This is not so with
the smaller summer sizes, unless the line is being
dragged. I have often landed a fish and found the
cast through the mouth and gills and the hook in

the side of the fish. The chewed fly had been ejected through the gills ; a clear proof that my line had no drag on it and was slack. The fish generally takes somewhere downstream of me.

Regarding the reason for striking, or rather tightening sooner with a big fly than a small one : in February and March, when I use a No. 1 to No. 4 fly, in strong water or even in low water, the fish come *so slowly* at the fly near the surface, that if you allow the fly to pass over them quickly, they will not move to it. I use greased line and keep the fly as near the surface as I can, and bring it over the fish so slowly that it is only just moving. To do this, I have to fish at the same angle as one would with a big, sunk fly, but I throw (or mend) the line outwards straight above the fly and keep on doing so if necessary, according to the strength of the current ; but let the fly come slowly across and slightly downstream. When the fish comes to the fly it is more or less in the same position as one would be that came at a sunk fly. Owing to this position, it is impossible to get the line to drop below the fish, so therefore, as soon as the fish goes down—and not before—I have to tighten quickly. Experience soon convinced me that, in cold weather, provided that the air was warmer than the water, greased line and a No. 1 hook would pay better than sunk fly provided one could fish it really slowly. I succeeded in doing this by switching (mending) over the greased line, always keeping it above the fly ; in other words, controlling the speed of the fly by the line, and I think this accounts chiefly for my success on days when others do not get any fish.

Directly the water gets warm and on the low side and fish are more lively, I use my ordinary method of letting the fly drift down and across, invariably letting the rod lead the line. In this way the fish hook themselves, but *then* I am fishing with smaller flies and the line pulls from below. If the fish are on the take, and keen for the fly, which is not often at this time of year, then I fish this way with No. 1 hook ; but as the barb is bigger on the No. 1, I tighten fairly sharply, though by no means a strike, in the generally-accepted sense of the word.

After you have made a cast, and when all is on the water to your satisfaction, lead the line with the point of the rod. The height of the rod-point above the water should vary with the strength of the stream and the size of the hook. With a No. 1 hook, hold the rod-point from three to six feet above the surface, the higher distance for a fast stream, the lower for a slack one. With a hook of No. 4 downwards, hold the point still higher, varying with the strength of the stream and the size of the fly, even as high as twelve feet or more when fishing in a very strong stream with a very small fly. Under all conditions, always keep the point higher with a short line than with a long one.

When a fish goes for the fly, continue moving the point of the rod round as if no fish were there. With the point of the rod three feet or less above the surface, move it round at the same level; when it is above three feet drop the point towards your own bank, but continue moving it. Do nothing more until you feel the fish, which will already have been hooked, because the stream has done the trick for you. If a fish misses the fly, I have often seen it come again; sometimes two or three times in the same cast, and finally hook itself (Fig. 6). This would not have happened if I had struck or pulled the line. As you are clearly seeing all this taking place in front of your eyes and are in consequence very apt to pull at the fly or increase its speed, keep your head and force yourself to pay no attention *until you feel the fish*.

Another difficult fish to hook is the one straight below you, or that takes the fly at the moment you begin to draw in line after a cast has been fished out. A salmon often takes you then, as though it thought the fly was trying to run away. There is a sudden snatch and grab, and it is often done like lightning. If you ask the old hand the most difficult fish to hook, he will say, " the one that takes straight below me." When you are using a small fly you can, to a great extent, overcome this trouble by fishing with your rod-point raised very high. This gives the fish a slack line. If the stream is *very* strong and I am using my twelve-foot rod, I sometimes hold the

latter perpendicularly. I hold it at this height in
order to give plenty of slack line in the air when,
owing to the pace of the current, there is no slack
in the water, and, whenever I see a fish or any movement near the fly, I at once drop my rod downstream
and towards my own bank. If this is done quickly
enough, the fish will have a slack line and can take
the fly and turn before it gets the pull ; and then the
drag of the line from below pulls the hook back into
the angle of the jaw. The result is generally a firmly-
hooked fish. I have been straight above a fish when
I hooked it, and on seeing the rise have dropped the
point of my rod towards my bank. In a second or so
I felt the pull of the line, and so did the fish, I found then
that the sooner I was out of the water the better, as I
frequently have had them come up with a rush straight
past me before I could move in the strong water.

I do not believe any fish intentionally comes short ;
the fault lies in the way we fish. When you are
fishing slow-moving water and have a very long line
out, keep the rod a foot or less above the surface ;
there will already be plenty of slack line on the
water. You may not be able to see the fly when
the fish takes it ; but, if you watch the line near
the cast, you will see it stop or being held. With
only a short line in slow water, keep the point of
the rod about three feet above the surface ; but in
fast streams, hold it very high, in order to get slack
by making a belly of line in the air. When you

see the fish take, drop the rod-point downstream towards your own bank. Do this quickly, and only then feel for your fish; more than likely it has already been hooked, and, thanks to the pressure of the current on the line, it is likely the hook has already been pulled home.

Some of my friends have tried holding slack line in the hand and letting it go as the fish takes; this helps, but the difficulty is to let it run out quickly enough, and that is why I prefer a belly of slack line in the air. Of course, in fast water, slack given from the hand, in addition to that caused by dropping the rod, is very useful. (Fig. 10.)

Handling the Loose Line

As to pulling in a long line and holding it in the left hand. If I am on rocks I coil the line at my feet or let it lie on the water, where it can lie fairly easily if it is greased; and if you remember that when you hook the fish the line is there and do not move your feet until the line has run out I do not think you will have any trouble. Sometimes, having hooked a very gentle taker, a fish that does not seem to realize it has been hooked, your trouble may begin. I always make up my mind to pay no attention to the fish on these occasions, I just hold the line on the rod with my left hand lightly enough to keep a certain tension without bending the rod except the tip, and start to reel up the line; if you

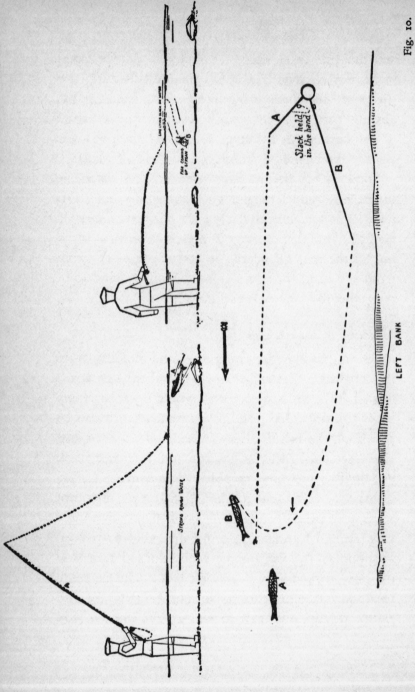

Fig. 10.

The Rod is held very high (A) so that if a fish takes the fly when it has arrived below you, slack may be given to avoid a break, by dropping the rod-point downstream and towards the bank (B).

have not moved your feet and there are no loose twigs you should be able to clear the line.

I once had an awful moment with a lot of loose line; the fish gave a run and before he had taken all the loose line out I got a half hitch round one of my fingers, but luckily the fish lay still for a moment and I got clear. If I am wading I find I can let a lot of line lie about in the water so long as I do not move; sometimes I get into trouble, but not often, as the stream straightens out the line, and keeps it clear for you.

Playing the Fish

I am always very careful to see that my reel runs freely. This precaution has saved me many broken casts and lost fish. Fishing with a light greased line often brings you into very direct touch with the fish. While you are playing a salmon as much as thirty or forty yards of line, or even more, may be in the air, so there is direct pull on the fish, and no sunk or sagging line to act as a spring or cushion. If you find this has happened, your first care should be to get part of the line into the water; it is far better, when light tackle is being used, to have a little of the line drowned than for all of it to be in the air. The reel line is fairly fine, so the current will not exert much pressure on any part of the line which is drowned.

I always play all my fish with the rod held side-ways and about horizontal, point downstream; and this I find by far the most effective method.

A sideways strain seems to hamper a fish's movements and generally results in tiring him more quickly than the usual way of playing with a raised rod. After all, there is little sense in continually pulling upwards as though you were trying to lift the fish out of the river; and it only makes him more determined to get his head down and fight hard. Besides, I like to have a bit of the line in the water to act as a safety buffer.

As to bringing a fish to the gaff; I think every fisherman should learn to gaff his own fish, not necessarily the first few, otherwise it will take him years to learn how to bring in a fish to the ghillie properly. I have seen so many fish brought in to the gaff at impossible angles, giving the ghillie no chance whatever and the fisherman usually curses his ghillie for not having tried to gaff it. If he had only learned to gaff his own fish he would know what was easy and what was not.

In my early days, when I gaffed my own fish, I was told to keep a couple of yards of loose line held under a finger of the left hand ready to let go when the fish was gaffed. My experience soon showed that this old idea was most dangerous; if I had to let go those two yards of line I invariably lost the fish. This loose line running out and then suddenly tightening causes a jerk which is fatal. I always let the fish take line directly off the reel, the check of which is set to suit the gut I am using.

Never attempt to lift a really big fish out of the water, but draw it to the surface and then in to

A. H. E. WOOD CASTING.

NOTICE THE POWER IN THE FORWARD STROKE.

Plates 6—7

A GOOD DAY AT CAIRNTON.

MAY 18TH 1923. 13 FISH. ANOTHER WAS CAUGHT AFTER THE PHOTOGRAPH
WAS TAKEN, MAKING 14 IN ALL TO MR. WOOD'S OWN ROD.

Top : A. H. E. WOOD WAITING FOR A RISE.

Bottom : THE RIVER AT WADING HEIGHT.

(AT " BANK HEIGHT," AS MR. WOOD CALLED IT, PRACTICALLY NO WADING IS NEEDED.)

the bank, but do not lift it out of the water until it has touched the bank. I have seen many a gaff pulled out or straightened by trying to lift a big fish that has any kick left in it. In fact, it would take a strong man to hold it at the end of the gaff if it were kicking, and I have seen the shaft of the gaff break even on the bank, and being hung properly. Thirty pounds on the move can do wonders!

Problems of Presentation

Through the kindness of the Publishers, I am able to present Mr. Wood's original sketches from the Lonsdale Library "Salmon Fishing" volume; and propose, for the benefit of the greased-line novice, to take each in turn, explaining to the best of my ability the way in which each situation should be confronted. First we have Fig. 11, a fairly usual problem, that of fishing the slack water on the far side of a strong run.

The angler, standing beside the run, casts across and slightly downstream to point 1. The natural sequence of events is for the fly to be drawn into position 2; but do not allow this to occur. As soon as the fly alights, make a mend upstream to 3, then follow the line with the rod so as to get into position 4 as soon as possible. By so doing, the fly has fished down the quiet water at the edge of the stream— and this is one of the favourite lies—from 1 to 3 in a more or less straight path, diagonally down and across. When using sunk fly, such a procedure would be almost

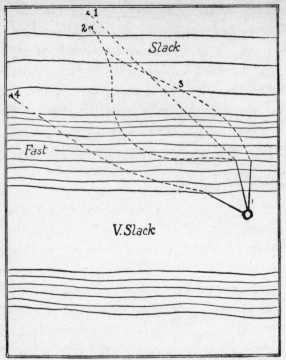

Fig. 11.
Cast to 1. Do not allow the line to get into position 2,
but mend it to 3 and prevent fly being pulled upstream.
Follow line round with rod so as to get position 4 as
soon as you can.

impossible, because the strong run would grip the
middle portion of the line and forcibly tear the fly out of
the quiet water, giving a fish no chance of taking it.

Figure 12 represents the exact reverse. Here the
fisherman is casting from slack water into fast.

In this case the fly is travelling faster than the
main line. Notice the reversed procedure; the line
has now to be lifted *downstream* in order to keep

pace with the fly. The fisherman casts to 1, and
holds his rod steady as the fly drifts from 1, through
2 to 3. By this time the line will be lagging behind
the fly, as shown in the sketch; therefore the fisherman mends downstream to 4, and then continues
slowly to move his rod to 5. If a slight tension is
maintained on the line, it will move faster, but drag
must be avoided at all costs. This particular problem

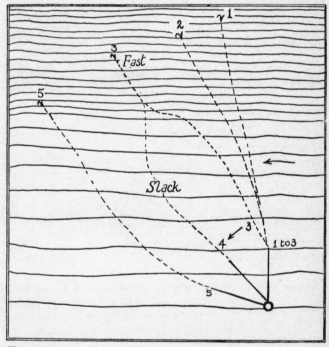

Fig. 12.

Cast to 1. By the time the fly gets to 3 there is an upstream belly in the line; correct this by mending to 4
and then continue to bring rod round to 5. Maintaining
tension on line will help to keep the line moving down
faster.

no doubt appears simple upon paper; but in actual practice a nice judgment is required as to the exact moment at which to mend the line. Further, the maintenance of the very slight tension while the fly is drifting from 3 to 5 is by no means as simple as might be imagined, but with practice it is soon

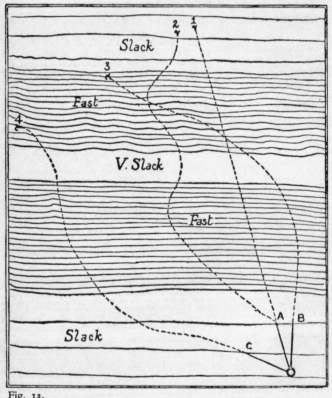

Fig. 13.

Cast to 1. Never let the line get into position 2 and keep on mending it so that it is in position 3 most of the time. When you get to 4 hold rod at C, and let the fast water pull the fly over the slack water.

mastered. In my own case, I had the inestimable advantage of personal tuition by Mr. Wood, and what a splendid teacher he was. So keen, and so delighted when he saw that you had grasped the point he was demonstrating.

Figure 13 shows a more complex problem: A cast from slack water across two streams with an intervening slack.

The fisherman makes his cast from A to point 1. If left to its own devices, the line would then become bellied in two places; i.e., the two fast streams, as shown at 2. The only way in which to fish the far slack, the farther stream and across the centre slack is to make a big mend upstream to B 3; if necessary, drawing some slack line off the reel and switching this out, and keep on mending, so that the fly fishes down and across as shown at 3.

Having fished to the nearest edge of the farther stream, hold the rod across to C, downstream, when the current will pull the fly across the slack and into the near stream, which you can easily fish. If the line drags, make a mend upstream.

Notice the delightful variations. This is the charm of greased-line fishing; it compels you to think! Each stream and eddy presents a new problem, so that even a blank day passes with the speed of thought. Concentration is vital, and the casual and inattentive fisherman who allows his fly to drag all over the river is missing ninety per cent. of the joy which successful greased-lining brings.

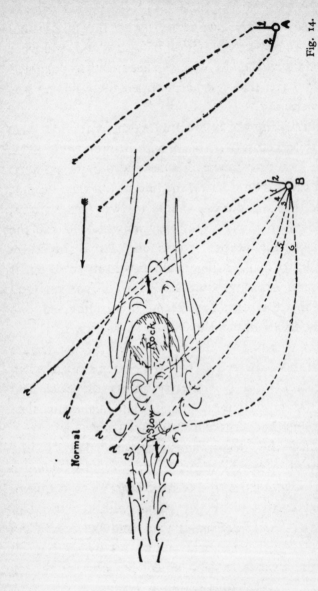

Fig. 14.

Shows how the difficult area beyond a band of quiet water can easily be covered. B1. Cast and mend to B2. Mend again from 3 to 4. Allow fly to be drawn gently from 5 to 6 by letting the rod swing round. Compare the diagram with Figure 15.

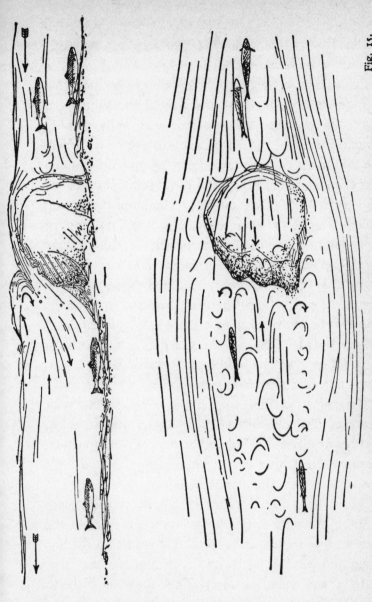

Fig. 15.

These show the way in which a fly can be sucked down behind a stone.

Finally, we come to the problem of the eddy behind the rock.

Look first at Fig. 15; it will be noticed that salmon lie both in front and behind the submerged rock. It will also be apparent that a fly passing over the rock is sucked down into the eddy, where the two fish shown on the left are lying. Incidentally, this sketch very clearly shows the extreme importance of keeping one's line out of eddies, for the strong down-draught of water holds the line in a grip of iron, and mending becomes impossible. Eddies are the chief bunkers which the greased liner encounters; many a good cast has been rendered nugatory by an unnoticed eddy. The fisherman then tries to mend the line, but finds that it is so tightly held that the fly is dragged yards. There is a certain similarity between bunkers in golf and eddies in greased-lining; and many a good round has been spoiled in both cases!

Returning to Fig. 14; the fish above the rock presents few difficulties. The angler stands at A, and his fly covers the fish as shown. When, however, he moves to B, his difficulties commence. Mr. Wood's remarks on this situation ran thus:

"In fishing an eddy behind a rock you can place a fly on the edge of the stream on the far side of the rock and, as soon as it has settled, you can lift the line again and place it upstream. (See Fig. 14, cast from B to 1 and mend to B2.) This allows the fly to wander about behind the rock and by the time the stream on your side of the rock has got hold of the line, so that you cannot lift again, you will most likely find the fly held by a fish. Often in this circumstance, you will not see the fish take the fly, as the latter has been sucked down by the back eddy, therefore, *watch the line*. You can continue all down that eddy, fishing in the same way and, as soon as you begin to cover the water below the rock, you will meet other fish, and very likely see one or two head-and-tail rises at the fly. In other words, as the fly gets further downstream from the influence of the eddy, it will keep on the surface instead of being sucked down, and so the rises will be visible. How far below the rock you can expect this to happen depends upon whether the rock is showing above the water or how deep its top is below, or how strong the current is. But this type of rise will often be observed near to the point where the two streams widen, converge and join the general flow, that is, where the water between them begins to move downstream and gets free of the influence of the eddy or reverse current."

Refer again to Fig. 14. Cast to B1 and mend to B2. Mend again from 3 to 4 and the fly is in the eddy. Then deliberately allow the current to draw the fly across the eddy by allowing the rod to swing from 5 to 6, when the fly comes almost square across the fish, but slightly upstream, as shown. On paper, no doubt, this appears rather complex, but in actual practice is fairly straight-forward.

I would advise the novice first to study the diagram until he knows it by heart, then hie him to the river, find a suitable rock and experiment. Fifteen minutes should suffice to show the principal snares. The chief difficulty lies in calculating the exact length of line nicely to present the fly in positions 5 and 6 ; usually one is inclined to over- or under-cast.

Summer & Low Water

Mr. Wood was fond of experimenting during the hot days of summer, when serious fishing was over for the year. He called this " fooling about " or " playing tricks " ; but much valuable information was gathered during these occasional hours at the waterside.

The Dee in summer, when the water is low, is absolutely crystal-clear, and affords wonderful opportunities for studying the way in which salmon respond to various devices for their undoing. One method tried was a scheme for inducing the fly to float awash during the entire cast. It has previously been mentioned that, in fine, hot weather, the cast should be made rather upstream, and the fly allowed to float on its side, when fish often take it. This circumstance suggested that it might be advantageous to keep the fly practically awash in hot weather.

The question of the shadows cast by the knots in the gut was also one for consideration—although as each ripple on the surface cast a shadow, Mr. Wood did not believe this to be a very vital factor. In order to kill two birds with one stone, he employed a cast of gut substitute, thereby eliminating the knots; and by greasing the cast for about half its length, ensured that the fly was always more or less on the surface. The ungreased portion soon became saturated with water and the fly was therefore awash during practically the whole of the drift; riding neither too high nor too low.

Mr. Wood, referring to what a salmon will, and will not, take said: " I have often had salmon take the floating knot which fastens the line to the cast, which annoys me pretty badly! One cannot help it though; they will take anything."

Regarding summer fishing also, Mr. Wood said:

" I am quite happy with fish which have been in the water a long time as it is then I think my method is the only one of much use, and I think it has been these stale fish which have caused my method to come so quickly to the front, as my neighbours soon found that I often had a very big bag of ten fish or more when none of them had touched a fish. This started the ball rolling.

" In low water, where fish have been lying a long time, weeks and months, if you fail with my method, try the pure dry-fly; that is, one of those big hackle flies the same as the Americans use. I am sure you will find that effective when no one else gets a fish. I do it occasionally, but more often I grease one of my ordinary flies and let it float; but

I would certainly first of all try ordinary greased line fly sunk just, and only just, beneath the surface."

In September, 1933, when the Dee was at drought-level, I received an object lesson. Mr. Wood was demonstrating his painted hooks, the " Redshanks " and " Blueshanks." These were fished exactly as any other small fly ; that is, cast slightly upstream on a greased line and allowed to fish down and across. The water being rather slow, and the hook small, the rod-point was held moderately high. At the third cast a fish rose and inspected, but did not touch the " fly." Three casts later he took the painted hook ; Mr. Wood dropped the rod-point ; the line bellied, and the fish was securely hooked. Then it was that I suggested the names " Redshank " and " Blueshank," and Mr. Wood, much amused, agreed to adopt them. He was, however, careful to point out that these hooks had not yet received an extended trial and that therefore he was not certain as to their general utility ; but he felt reasonably confident that salmon would take them in any height of water.[1]

If, as the result of trial by other fishermen, it is found that these hooks will take fish as well as ordinary flies what becomes of the carefully cherished theories of the fly-dressers ? When any soulless bungler with a pot of cellulose paint and a brush can dress his own lures in a minute of time, and

[1] Personally, I cannot imagine many anglers having sufficient pluck to use them ; they would fear lost opportunities.

find them dry and ready for use in a few more minutes —cellulose being very quick-drying—where will the expert tyers be then ? Where, O ! Where ? Mr. Wood revolutionized the process of fishing the fly; is he destined to bring about a still more sweeping change —the abolition of feathers, tinsel, silk *et hoc genus omne ?* I wonder! I should, I think, make it clear that these experiments were usually carried out over potted fish after the spring run—and serious fishing —was over.

As his experience grew, Mr. Wood insisted more and more strongly upon the importance of cutting down the dressing of flies for use in low water and beneath a strong sun. His summer flies consisted of an almost bare hook and two or three hairs of hackle; therefore the " Blueshanks " and " Redshanks " were the logical outcome of this tendency.

These painted hooks, I again repeat, are fished exactly as are the ordinary flies ; in hot weather they should be cast rather more upstream than square across and allowed to drift down in the usual way.

The " toys " mentioned in the chapter on tackle were fished in fast water, as a rule, with the rod-point held well up in the air, ready to give slack should a fish rise to the fly. They possessed the great advantage of not skirting, and fish were hooked on them on several occasions.

Regarding fishing from jetties in hot weather, shooting and paying out line until forty or fifty yards were out and letting it drift down, Mr. Wood firmly believed in the efficacy of this proceeding, for, as he said: " The longer the line the slower will the fly cross, and the progressively lengthening casts give you a gradually diminishing speed ; therefore a fish which has seen the fly pass fairly quickly may be tempted into taking it by the slower speed of subsequent casts. Of course, you will lift and mend the line if it shows any sign of dragging."

Generally speaking, in hot summer weather, it pays to cast rather upstream, allow the fly to float until the line tightens, then jerk it under the surface if it still persists in floating, and fish it down and round as usual ; remembering always to keep slack line in the air and on the water ; and to use a very small and thinly-dressed fly or a painted hook.

MISCELLANEOUS TIPS

An Upstream Wind

A wind, blowing contrary to the general flow of the water, makes it very easy to lift the line upstream in mending. Further, another very important point is that an upstream wind checks the line and keeps it from travelling downstream too fast, which helps you to fish more slowly and to control the fly more easily.

A Downstream Wind

A strong downstream wind is always awkward for the greased-liner ; even the expert finds it difficult to lift against it. The only way is to hold back the point of the rod and not follow the line so much and then make little lifts upstream whenever you can manage them between the puffs of wind. If you can wade, much of the trouble is avoided by fishing more downstream and keeping above the fish instead of nearly abreast of them—the normal position.

To find the right size of Fly

To find the right size of fly I often start by fishing big, watching carefully and, if I find I have moved a fish, putting on a small fly. When there are kelts about and it is a stiff day, I put on a small fly and fish for kelts; when I get one or move one, I put up a fly a few sizes bigger and very often get a fresh fish. This is the way I fish on stiff days and I find it very useful. As a matter of fact, as long as the fish will take the larger sized (No. 1 to No. 4) flies I stick to them; but if a fish comes and looks at the fly and turns away then I put on a smaller fly until I get the size they will come to *without any hesitation. The colder the water, the bigger the fly;* that is my experience. I do not use a smaller hook than I can help, but you must remember that the fly proper, the body, wings, etc., is smaller than the hook. Of course the idea of using as big a hook as the fish will take is that it gives you more chance of landing him. (Mr. Wood to a friend.)

The Time to Fish with the Greased Line

Many people seem to think that surface fishing is no use, except in shallow water and during hot weather. Experience has shown me that it is equally good in icy water, as long as the *air is warmer than the water*. It is also good in all depths of pools, if the water is reasonably clear. My favourite pool in February and March is a slack water on the edge of a strong stream, and that pool is twelve to fifteen feet deep. At that time of the year I usually use a No. 1 hook. Later in the season and in warm weather, the fish lie in the strong stream of this pool, and deep as it is they often take a summer hook No. 8. Every day I fish, even in February, I start by using a greased line and only when it fails do I use a sunk line and a big fly. As a result my fishing book shows that forty-three per cent. of my fish caught in February in the last ten years were taken on greased line and small fly, sixty-five per cent. in March, ninety-four per cent. in April, and ninety-eight in May, and so on. I used to think it was no good fishing the greased line and small fly except in warm weather; but some years ago on the opening day, the 11th February and very cold, by late afternoon my sunk line was frozen up in the rod-rings. As a last hope to end a good day's fishing, I tried a greased line and small fly No. 1 hook, as the greased line does not freeze up so quickly, and managed to get two more fish.

That made six; four on big fly and two on greased
line, the last two both caught after four o'clock.
Since then I have always fished greased line in all
weathers and under all conditions, even in snowstorms, and it rarely fails or is beaten by a sunk
line; but I like to know that the *air is a bit warmer
than the water*. In early Spring when the temperature
of the water is more often under thirty-eight degrees
Fahrenheit, that of the air is generally higher. On
the other hand, the air may well be colder than the
water on a May evening, when the water is as much
as sixty degrees and over. This does seem to put the
fish down. I use, therefore, a big fly under those
conditions; and this accounts for the occasional
fish caught by me on a big fly, as late as April and
even May.

In hot weather during May, June or July, when
the water is really warm, it pays always to cast across
and upstream and to let the fly float and drift down,
as it likes, and at times to lift the line upstream to
prevent drag. For three-quarters of the distance
travelled the fly will float on the surface, practically
dry. You will get a lot of fish to take the fly in this
position, although it lies flat on the surface and not
cocked up like a dry fly riding on the tips of its
hackles. When the line reaches its full extension
downstream and across the fly may skim across the
surface of the water, leaving a wake behind it. Never
let this occur; as soon as the line tightens, give it

a jerk, which will put the fly under water, you can then fish it round to your own bank.

There appear to be two almost-distinct periods when salmon have different ways of taking the fly. Until the water and the air get continuously warm (say fifty-five degrees or over), the fish do not come freely to the drifting-down or dry fly. Therefore when fishing early in the year, do not waste time casting upstream or even square across; but put the fly rather more upstream than is usual in orthodox methods. Occasionally try the upstream or square-across cast as you never know what a salmon will do. If the fish start taking the floating fly, continue the upstream cast, as there is nothing more deadly than the use of a floating fly and the practice of dibbing for salmon. We do not often get the right weather in this country at the time the fresh fish are up. If we did, we should get more fish than we actually want to give us good sport.

Odds & Ends

It is, I think, just possible that the point of tightening sideways when a fish takes has not been sufficiently emphasized. This is really one of the most vital points in the whole method. I would ask the reader to refer to Fig. 16.

First: it is necessary for the novice to realize that, when fishing greased line, his line is, or should be, much more across stream than is practicable or

usual when fishing sunk fly. Second: when the
fish takes, the line bellies, and this belly is, of course,
dragging on the surface of the water. Mr. Wood
has given ample instruction as to affording the
necessary amount of slack by dropping the rod-
point, but he has said very little on the importance
of keeping the line on the water. In conversation
with me, however, he again and again stressed this
feature of his method. The upright strike would

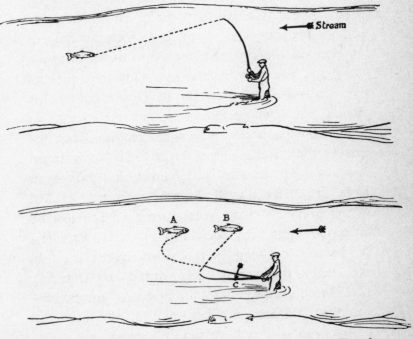

Fig. 16.

Hooking a fish on the greased line. Note that rod is
kept low (bottom), while in top picture the angler is
shown wrongly striking overhead. Compare the two.

lift the dragging belly of line off the water and thereby alter the angle of pull from downstream to upstream and, in the process, very probably pull the hook out of the salmon's mouth. By keeping the rod more or less horizontal and swinging it towards the bank, the angle of pull is kept as far downstream as may be. Again, notice that it is only the cast and a small portion of the line which actually bellies, and when you tighten, you draw taut merely this comparatively small curve.

Seeing that the whole point of the method, its leading, mending and so on, is to secure a hold in the angle of the jaw, it is foolish to throw away the advantage you have gained by deliberately striking overhead—the sure way in which to nullify the trouble you have previously taken! At the risk of being voted a bore I will again repeat: keep the line on the water; tighten horizontally downstream and towards your own bank, and do it slowly—you have, in most cases, all the time there is! As Mr. Wood says: "I have seen dozens of fish lost by trying to tighten too quickly; but very, very few by waiting too long." If possible, ignore the fish, and carry the rod steadily round, remembering Mr. Wood's advice as to the height of the point— dropping it when necessary—and, in nine cases out of ten, your fish will be solidly hooked.

Par exemple, I once saw a friend hook a fish in this way while entirely unconscious of what was

happening. His fly was drifting and his rod well
downstream and fairly low, the water being easy.
A shout from behind caused him to turn his head,
when, at the identical moment, a fish took the fly,
tightened the line itself, and was beautifully hooked
in the angle of the jaw !

Fish " Coming Short "

Mr. Wood did not believe in this time-honoured
excuse : " The more I fish, the more I am convinced
I am right on this point, and when it is possible—
and that is very often—I see where I am at fault
when I have pulled a fish. Then I blame myself
for not having put the fly right or had enough slack
line to prevent the fish feeling the pull—in other
words, let the fish turn before he felt the hook.
From what I see, the fish seem to hold these small
flies very loosely in their mouths, and if the pull
is forward it invariably comes out. But if proper
time is given, if you do get a hold it is always at the
back of the mouth at one side or the other and has
a firm hold. Of course, there are times when the
hook slips through and the point never touches.
This you usually feel, but I do not call that ' coming
short.' There are days when fish are sluggish and
come at the fly more lazily ; then you must give
them more time to turn. Those are the days when
most of us get what we call ' coming short,' for
the reason that the current or we ourselves have

tightened on the hook before the fish has turned
or closed his mouth."

Days when a fish will not take

Mr. Wood wrote: "I do not believe that a
salmon is immovable to-day and will take to-morrow.
If the fisherman is good enough the fish will take
any day, at least one should not have a blank. One
does have plenty of blanks, but it is the fisherman's
own fault. However, I do agree that there are days
when they are difficult, and as far as my knowledge
goes, impossible; and there are also days when
anyone can get a fish with anything—a bit of wool
tied on to a string will even serve. I know that
changing water even to the extent of only $\frac{1}{8}$ inch
rise immediately means fish; in fact, it is all these little
changes of temperature in the air, a glimpse of sunshine
or movement of water that just make all the difference.

"The longer I fish, the more I am beginning to
think that getting fish has very little to do with
conditions; what I do find important is the way
you put the fly over the fish. I used to think I could
always get fish in certain spots under certain conditions of weather and water; but I now find that
at any height of water, if you can fish it properly,
you will get a fish. Naturally, I am talking generally,
not of any particular pool that could hold fish one
time and not another; in fact, regarding what Kelson
said about noting the conditions under which you

catch fish and then applying the same methods when the conditions recur, I am afraid I do not agree with it, although perhaps six years ago I would.

"How often in a man's life will you get exactly the same conditions in a certain spot? Personally, I should say *never*. There would always be one of a dozen things different. I quite agree that certain pools fish better at certain heights of water, but if they are pools, whatever the height, they are always fishable, though possibly in a different way."

Summary

Possibly a brief summary of the principal points to be borne in mind may be found helpful; to the beginner at all events.

In cold water on the heavy side

Use a No. 1 to No. 4 hook.

Cast a slack line more or less square across, let it drift down; when the line tightens, lead with the rod-point.

Mend the cast as often as necessary.

Let the fly drop as much downstream as possible, i.e., as much down as across.

As the fly reaches a position almost straight downstream, keep the rod behind (upstream of) the line to avoid a pull on the straight rod.

Raise rod while pulling in line ready for the next cast, and if a fish comes for the fly, drop the point.

Always try to present a sideways view of the fly.

Fish as slowly as possible. If the fly is coming down too fast, mend—and keep on mending—upstream.

When a fish takes, drop the rod-point downstream towards your own bank.

In slow water, hold rod about a foot above the surface.

In strong water the rod-point should be about three feet above the surface; and in very strong water above the head with some slack line in the left hand ready to pay out in addition to dropping the rod-point.

In warm weather and low water

Use No. 6 to No. 12 hook.

Have plenty of slack on the water and in the air.

Under these conditions, the strike can be postponed almost indefinitely, as fish will hold the very small fly for a long time. Cast rather more upstream and allow fly to float until the line tightens, then jerk it under.

At all times, and under all conditions, avoid drag as you would the plague.

Concentrate on the line, and never allow your attention to be distracted. Lack of concentration is one of the novice's chief faults.

Never, under any circumstances, strike overhead. This is the most fatal error of all!

CHAPTER FIVE

ASKED & ANSWERED

MR. WOOD constantly received letters asking for advice upon salmon fishing matters. As time passed and his reputation increased, this correspondence increased in volume until, in later years, he had literally hundreds of letters. In the case of the more interesting queries it was his habit to file a carbon copy of his replies, and it is from this source that the present chapter has been compiled. It will be found in certain cases that the replies are somewhat similar in their wording; this arises from Mr. Wood's habit of repeating the same terms and phrases in different letters, and rather than change his wording—and I am sure that his personal friends especially would greatly prefer to read his exact opinions word for word—I have made little attempt to edit these letters. To do so would be to spoil Mr. Wood's style, which, to my mind, is far more interesting, informal and characteristic of the man himself than any result which my own bungling efforts could produce. I have, however, endeavoured to re-arrange some few sentences of which the purport appeared to be not quite clear—

due, doubtless, to their being dictated rather hurriedly, for Mr. Wood was, as I have said, an extremely busy man. Some attempt at classification has been made, but the task has not been easy, due to the fact that many querists wrote concerning several different topics at the same time. I would ask the reviewers, therefore, to be merciful, and to spare a kindly thought for the Editor trying to do his best! Again, it is possible that the critical eye will discover a certain amount of repetition, which is difficult to avoid. The arrangement which appeared to be most suitable was to classify the queries under the headings : " Weather and conditions "; " Sunk fly "; " Greased line proper "; and " Miscellaneous," which latter includes such matters as the habits of salmon and tackle.

Weather and Conditions

1. If your question means do I prefer the sun shining directly downstream, I *do* like it; but if at an angle across the stream so that the fly travels between the sun and the fish, then I certainly do not like it.

2. As to the temperature of the atmosphere affecting sport with the greased line, the answer is very simple : when the air is colder than the water sport is bad; and when the air is warmer than the water it is good.

3. You ask whether a frosty night affects sport on the following day. In my experience, sport is generally good as soon as the air becomes warm.

4. I think that the state of the moon has a bearing on the matter of catching fish. Fish seem to run freely when the moon is up, especially with a rising water; but I have found it quite useless to fish in the evening when the moon begins to affect the daylight.

5. I like fine, hot weather, with plenty of strong sun, or, failing sun, at least a strong light.

6. You ask if I prefer to fish before or after a flood. I like the first hour or so; just when the water commences to rise. The third day after the spate is generally good unless the peat has been coming down, in which case the fish seem to be sick for some considerable time.

7. I don't like a brown water, but there is always a chance if it isn't too " peasoupy."

8. I don't care for a lot of white cloud in the sky, but if there is plenty of sunshine I don't think it matters much.

9. I always like an upstream wind because it helps to check the drift of the line and makes it easier to switch line upstream.

10. You ask if fog affects the fishing. I have no experience of pukka fog, but a Scotch mist, and also an east wind, if warm, will produce good sport.

11. My charts show that there is no special time of day at which salmon take. All hours are equal except possibly on a stiff day the last twenty minutes of daylight, there again only if conditions are

ordinarily good. The Cairnton records show no favourite hour except those controlled by weather, that is, with a cold morning and a warm afternoon you would get fish in the afternoon, and other conditions like that. Equable weather makes an equal fishing day. In February and March after a frosty morning, the first hour in which the sun warms things up is perhaps the time when everyone may get a fish, or at least have a chance or two. There is always a peak period in the morning between 11 and 12 noon, and an equally high peak in the evening or afternoon.

Of course, we lunch at 1 o'clock, and there is always a drop between 1 and 2 o'clock. If we all fished straight through, no doubt the line on the chart from 1 o'clock to 3 o'clock would remain level. I don't think there is any special time of day at which fish take best—so much depends upon temperature variations.

12. The lowest water temperature at which I fish greased line and small fly is about 39° or 40°, but if there is a very cold wind I use a big fly and sink it.

13. Why do salmon refuse a surface-fishing fly when the air is colder than the water? They will not put their noses out under these conditions. I had a clear case of this lately. The last week in March and all the first three weeks in April we had nothing but strong N.W. gales and it was very

cold. The air temperature was hardly ever above
40°, generally under, but owing to the sun, although
we did not feel the effect of it, the shallow water did
and it was generally a few degrees warmer than the
air. This I tested most days when out fishing at all
hours besides the morning and evening temperatures,
which I took and booked regularly every day. During
this time we were hardly getting a fish a day. Then
we had a white world for two days, with 12° to 14°
of frost every night. The water got low and cold and
the highest temperature in the morning was 38°, but
although we had all this snow, and cold gales from
the N.W., the air temperature was still about 40° to
42° during the day, while the water remained about
38° to 40° during the day. The result was that we
caught thirty fish in the week out of ninety-one for
the whole month.

This is a very clear instance as we had exactly the
same conditions, and the last week was even colder
than the previous, *but* the water was colder than
the air. The month of the year has nothing to do
with it. You get exactly the same conditions in
May and June with a higher temperature in both
cases, but with the air colder than the water. This
immediately puts the fish down, in fact, the fish
appear to demand a bigger difference in temperature
between the air and the water, i.e., the air needs
to be *much* warmer than the water to produce a really
tip-top fishing day.

In February, the air must be warmer than the
water; and if it is only 2° warmer than the water
you will still get fish. If the air is colder than the
water you do not. As to why it affects the fish in
this way, of course, one can only guess; but this is
my idea. You would not put your nose outside the
door in such weather unless you had to for the sake
of health or otherwise. Also, I suppose, there must
be something to do with air pressure under those
conditions. But even if you sink a big fly down to the
bottom amongst the fish they do not take it readily,
though it is your only chance of catching fish at all.
It seems to numb the fish and take all the life out of
them. There is no doubt that fish are very susceptible
to temperature and pressure-changes. On days such
as I have mentioned with excessive differences in the
temperature, water warm and air cold, I have not seen
either bait or fly do well.

Some people say that a cool air is good for sport.
Personally, I don't believe it; I should say exactly the
opposite, for the hotter the day the better the sport
—that has always been my experience. You cannot
compare a salmon in a river to the same, or any other,
fish in the sea because the sea is not affected by the air
in the same way as is the river, nor is the water so
deep in the river, so the two cannot be compared.

I might also point out that, in cold weather, bait
fishing—either artificial or natural—does no better
than fly.

14. You ask where the fish lie during low water in cold weather. Some of them lie on the edge of the strong water, but the great majority seem to be lying in three to four feet of water with a fair amount of stream. Quite a number lie in the strong water behind stones, quite different to what they do when the water is high and cold. You have to keep the fly moving slowly and in the stream hang it over them and give them time to come up to it.

15. You say you think that the fish did not touch your fly because it went for the shadow of the fly instead of the fly itself. I hardly think that this can be right as, however bad the sun, I think a fish knows what a shadow is and would never go for it. At the same time, I do think the sun at a certain angle does prevent them seeing the fly, or the shadow distracts their attention as it is approaching, as if I move a fish with the sun at that angle, I find if he takes the fly at all, he does so after it has passed him (the fish). As that means a snap at the fly you so often get only a pull and fail to hook.

The position of the sun that I hate most is such that your fly travels down the rays of the sun, that is, between the fish and the sun. If the sun is low in that quarter I have found it hopeless to fish at all. But when the sun is shining directly down the water facing the fish I have often had good sport.

16. With regard to the difficulty of catching fish after they have been a long time in fresh water. I

would not put it down to his losing all desire for food, but that the temperature of the water is so high that he has difficulty in breathing, and as food is not necessary to him he does not trouble to exert himself. This is, of course, a difficult question, but I think my idea is as likely to be true as any other.

17. You ask how long a flood puts the fish off their food. It all depends on the nature of the country. A peat flood, I find, sickens the fish for a good three days. If it is a case of road washings only then I think it is worth fishing when about half clear.

18. As to the lie of fish in cold weather, you will find them in the dead water and near the bottom, but never in very streamy water. In summer their favourite place is in shallow water at the tail or head of a pool, or in streamy places where they can get near the surface. If there are shallows in the pool the fish will be there in hot summer weather.

19. Do salmon change their quarters from winter to summer? Yes: In Spring, and for as long as the weather remains cold, you will find them in the deepest and quietest water. As the season advances and everything warms up they gradually move into the deeper water that has a stream; and about April—unless there are hard frosts or melted snow coming down the river—they work into the streamy water where it is shallow—say from three to six feet deep.

Sunk Fly

20. Yes : I think that a quick rising fish should be struck hard and quickly *if* he rises on to the surface. A salmon that suddenly comes at the fly and snatches it—and misses—generally stops dead and drifts backwards downstream or sinks to the bottom. On the whole I think it is a mistake to get into this habit of quick striking ; but in this case, i.e., where a fish makes a lightning dash at a fly, it may help to hit him quickly.

21. You ask how to make a big fly sink in heavy water. I would cast straight across, perhaps slightly upstream and throw a slack line especially near the fly, then lift the nearer part of the line and put it upstream as often as I can without interfering with the fly or the slack line near it. This gives it a chance to get well down towards the bottom. If possible, I like to drop the fly into a bit of slack water below a stone, and when I can no longer mend the cast, I let it drift down before putting on pressure with the rod. By this I mean letting the rod-point drop downstream according to circumstances : I might have the rod up all the time, dropping it as it goes round so as to let the fly downstream as far as possible and get over the question of drag. I do everything to prevent a pull by letting the whole outfit go as slack as possible. The fly is drifting down, but it is being worked by the eddies and is quite alive, for

I have seen fish take me in all positions, even meeting the fly as it drops on to the water ! Of course, if there is no chance of mending—and sometimes it is impossible with an ungreased line—you must cast more downstream, throwing a very slack line and hoping that the fly will sink as deep as you require before the line tightens. Another way is to cast downstream and give the fly and line a jerk when it is all on the water to get it all under quickly. This straightens things out, and, if done with the rod rather upstream, by following downstream with the rod-point the line sinks.

22. About fish following the sunk fly across the river. I certainly agree that they do follow ; but it is usually caused by a faulty way of presenting the fly. If the fly had been presented properly there would be no need for him to chase it, and also it would have looked natural enough for him to take it. I think that, in nine cases out of ten, the fish is following the dragging fly and wondering what it is, and wondering also why it is dashing about in that unnatural manner.

Greased Line

23. How much drag is permissible ? That depends upon circumstances ; but there should be as little as possible. You should be able to tell by the feel of the rod if there is any drag, even with your eyes shut. Even in fastish water you should be able to take your

hand off the line and none of it should run out through the rod-rings. You should feel no weight on the rod at all—let everything be perfectly free and slack.

24. With regard to your question about the greased line being no good in very narrow rivers. I first began fishing this way on a very narrow stream, and later I fished the North and South Ugie, and that is a mere ditch in parts. Some of it is not more than ten feet across and parts only six feet between the rushes, while most of it is very dead water ; but even there I managed to get more fish than anyone else had done. The greased line is there to keep the fly near the surface, therefore it does not matter what size of water. Very often in a big pool there is perhaps only one lie, and that is the only bit you trouble to fish. Now very likely this spot would be no larger than your narrow stream is, so where is the difference ? A short line makes no difference ; in fact I often prefer to use it instead of a long one. I have caught fish within six feet of my legs.

25. To answer your query about the best way to fish a very narrow stream, I think I had better tell you of my experiences on the North Ugie. The width varied from one and a half yards to fifteen to twenty yards, the average being about twelve yards. Most of it was like a canal. I had the shooting there and the water had the reputation of holding big fish, but no one had fished it for years. None of the keepers knew anything about it so it was all blind

water to me. The fish very rarely showed, so I had
no idea where they lay. It was what we call up there
" blackwater," but really very clear except that it had
a black, peaty bottom. Where it was wide enough
I cast downstream close to the other side and made a
belly in the line towards my own bank by switching
over, and then by keeping the rod over my bank
downstream. If the stream was not strong enough
to fish the fly I brought it across and slightly upstream
by pulling the line. This was effective and could
be varied according to the water. As a rule, if there
was not much stream, I pulled the line, but very
gently.

If I saw any indication of a move from a fish or
it looked a likely spot, I would give a second cast,
pulling the fly quicker ; but one dodge I had was
to use rather a big fly, say one and a half inches instead
of half-inch or threequarters-inch. With this bigger
fly I would often get the fish to move but not to take
it ; but that was all I was aiming at, to find where
the fish were. If I moved a fish like that I would at
once change to smaller fly and invariably got him.

In other places, especially if I had seen a fish, I
would stalk him and dap for him, that is always
deadly. By dapping I mean fishing with a small fly
and keeping it just touching the water, sometimes
hopping, sometimes just skimming, but very slowly.
The point of the rod, of course, up in the air with a
very short line ; in fact no belly in the line at all. If

I could only cover the water, the only time the line would be bellied would be if there was a stream.

In these narrow waters, and with fine tackle, I find it more difficult to get the fish after I have hooked him, as you can only go up and down the river in very narrow water and crooked banks. Many a time I have played a fish round the corner with my line under the bank, running for all I was worth and trying to clear it. Luckily the banks were only mud and grass.

You say you think the warmth of the water draws the fish into these narrow streams. Would it not be possible that the water has more oxygen in it, and the fish are after that?

If the banks are clear and you can throw a long line, you might try fishing upstream and drawing the fly. I think it might pay. Also, in such waters, if you can use a dry fly such as La Branche uses—a big hackle fly—I would certainly try it in hot weather and fish it just as you would do for trout. If it is summer time such as June or July, I think you would find it great fun. Do not be frightened at a little drag ; I would cast again and pull the fly in little jerks, but not too quickly, and you will be surprised how they go for it. If our conditions here were better I should have tried to improve the fly so as to enable the hook to go home, for the hackle seems to protect it. That has always been my difficulty with these big, hackle dry-flies—the fish take it well, but I can't hook them.

I am talking of really hot weather in June or July when our fish, having been up so long, get sluggish and do not seem to close their mouths on the fly properly.

26. You ask if it is worth fishing greased line and small fly in deep, slow-running water. Certainly it is; the only difference is that you fish it rather differently. You can afford to keep the point of the rod quite low when in slack water, but in fast streams the point must be well up in the air, so as to get a slack line in the air. The fish is hooked long before you know anything about it, and as the rod-point is well up you stand no risk of breaking the fine cast.

27. If I see a fish I always take up my position either just abreast of it, or a little above. So much depends upon the temperature and as to whether fish are taking well : if they are, then I do not mind being above them, in fact I prefer fishing across and dropping my fly slightly above the fish. I then let it drift down with a slack line.

In this cold weather they will not come up to a fast-moving fly, therefore I have to fish downstream in the orthodox manner, although most of my casts are made square across and are allowed to drift down and then across in the usual manner, hoping to get a fish as it drifts down. By doing this I cover a great deal more water than the ordinary method does ; perhaps twice as much.

28. You ask how much slack line I leave on the water. If I am using No. 1 to No. 6 hooks I do not aim at much, if any, slack line, I generally try to keep the line fairly straight; slightly curved but not dragging, and the rod-point near the surface, or slightly raised according to the pace of the current. This gives just enough line to allow the fish to turn before he feels the drag or strike, as *with a heavy hook* I tighten quickly as the fish feels the hook and gets rid of it as soon as he can. But when using small flies I give lots of slack because the fish hold on to the smaller hook for a much longer time.

29. As to Autumn fishing. I do not do much of it myself, but some of my friends do, and they, like myself, find it more deadly in the Autumn than at any other time (compared with ordinary fishing), but in the Autumn the fish will take slightly bigger flies. Personally, I shall be using No. 1 to No. 4 in Autumn, and as the fish do not seem to notice the cast so much at that time of year I always use heavier gut.

30. You say that you find a long line sinks and so, therefore, does the fly. That has not been my experience. I find that the whole line floats well enough, and generally most of the cast, whatever the distance thrown—and I generally fish from twenty-five to thirty yards. Very often the cast will float and the line will sink. Any good line should float if well greased, and it is surprising how it keeps up even in

rough water. Be sure that the line is dry before you grease it.

31. No : I very seldom use two flies ; but when I do I use a big one on the tail end of the cast to act as an " anchor," with a small dropper which I skim on the surface. The salmon seem to like the dancing dropper and leave the big tail fly alone.

32. Regarding greased line in a big flood. I have tried No. 1 hook on greased line in floods when the water was so thick you could not see more than an inch or two below the surface, and I find that even then the fish both see and take it. As a matter of fact I have had as many on small as I have on big, sunk flies. The reason why I do not always fish greased line in floods is that one uses light tackle with greased line and this is hardly suitable for flood conditions ; so when fishing in a big spate I use my heavy gear and big hooks, otherwise I might end up in Aberdeen in tow of the fish, unless I risked a break ! It does seem to me extraordinary how the fish can see the little fly in thick water—one would think it quite impossible—but in all waters except a really big flood I invariably fish small fly and greased line.

33. You ask about fishing greased line in very slowly-running water. As you say, there is nothing for it but to pull the line in slowly by hand to keep the fly moving. You mention pulling the fly in little jerks. Have you tried pulling it in at an even speed without jerks, as far as possible ? I sometimes find

the salmon seem a bit shy of the jerking fly, unless it is just one jerk when the fly is over the fish's nose. Then, I think it looks as if the fly had seen the fish and was trying to escape; and sometimes when trying for a stiff fish this little dodge has proved successful.

34. You say that fish sometimes come to meet your fly as it floats down. I consider that when they are doing that you are fishing perfectly; so all you have to do is to try and imitate your own methods again. If a fish comes like that he is invariably firmly hooked. If you can continue to persuade fish into meeting the fly you need no advice from me—you are doing capitally.

35. You ask if I can tell you of a trick to stir up a stiff fish lying in the tail of a pool. It is not a bad dodge, at the tail of a pool in glassy water, to let the fly down behind the fish and then suddenly draw it quickly up stream past him—sometimes he will have a go for it.

36. You ask about the fly and cast floating when you don't want them to and how to get over it. You will find in practice that if you allow it, especially in warm weather, the grease from the line gets on to the cast and fly, not only from your fingers after handling the line, but also when you are walking along the bank with your fly hooked on to the reel, as then the greasy line and the cast rub together. Rub the cast with a bit of dead grass to get the grease

off, and if it still floats, give the line a jerk, which will send the fly under water.

37. Regarding how a fish comes to the fly. He does not make a quick, sharp rise at it, but comes at it slowly, and, having taken the fly, drifts on upstream but slightly away from you towards the far bank. If you are fishing properly this will *invariably* happen and makes it easy to hook the fish as the cast and line are left behind and the current is also pulling them downstream; therefore, by the time you feel the pull the cast is lying lengthways with the fish.

There are times when the fish takes the fly after it has passed him and of course in this case the fly is generally level or below the fish and on your side of it. Under these conditions the fish does make a snap at it because he wants to turn his head upstream again as quickly as he can. The only thing to do is to give slack line immediately, otherwise the result is merely a pull—or a tear-out—or the old, old story of "the fish came short!" Poor fish! how they are libelled!

38. You see many fish taking your fly, but only prick them. That is very commonly the case with beginners. The fish come more freely to the fly, but owing to the fisherman seeing the fish or allowing the line to drag he pulls or pricks a lot of fish. As an ordinary rule the touch is so slight that I find fish come again very soon afterwards, sometimes

immediately; but if I prick a fish I look for it in an hour or two and try again—they soon forget. If you can only school yourself into leaving the line alone until you feel the fish—wait until the fish has disappeared—and don't allow any drag, you will soon be able to hook them.

39. In reply to your question, yes: I have seen fish play with the fly in all kinds of ways. I have seen the fly floating and the fish come up with more than a quarter of his length out of the water, fall on the fly to drown it, and then turn round and take it under water. This has occurred quite often, and when they do so they usually keep their mouths shut.

40. About short-rising fish. I contend that there is no such thing, and I am afraid that your argument does not convince me. Short-rising, so called, is not really a case of the fish coming short at all. What really happens is that the line is under tension—you are pulling it away—and you have not given the fish a chance of taking it as he would like to, so he has to follow it and take it from behind. If the fly were alive and not tied to a line he would not have come short of it, but, having taken it into his mouth, would have turned like a flash. Owing, however, to your fly being tightly held by the line, you are pulling one way and the fish the other, hence the pricks and misses. Suppose you are putting a fork full of food into your mouth and someone unexpectedly pulls your fork away just as you are

going to shut your mouth? That is exactly the same. You would " come short " at most of the mouthful, and would probably be just as surprised as the fish is!

41. You ask whether I like fishing a long line and find it pays? Yes, I certainly do. Of course, with my small flies, and always allowing a lot of slack line in hot weather, I find that fish hold on to the fly for quite a time and hook themselves. That is where my method differs from Hewitt's and La Branche's. I generally fish twenty-five to thirty yards and do not have to strike—in the usual sense of the word—but they fish about fifteen to twenty yards and are obliged to strike, because of the stiff hackle flies they use. If they fished a very long line they would not, I think, be able to get in the slack quickly enough to strike before the fish had rejected the fly. In my case, the fish holds on to the fly, so I can have any amount of slack line on the water; could even turn round and talk politics after I saw the fish come to the fly, and when I had finished I should expect the fish to be hooked! Some of my friends have said this as a joke, but it is really correct; so do not worry about fishing a long line because it will make no difference to the hooking of fish if you are fishing properly.

42. You say the greased line does not work in some waters. That surprises me because I have letters from all over the world saying how well it has done, and this is the first time that I have heard

of the method failing in anything like suitable weather. Even in Norway it is doing well on those heavy rivers there : and from Newfoundland, New Brunswick, England, Scotland, Ireland and Wales— even New Zealand for rainbow trout—I have received letters from men who say how much better sport they have had by adopting my method. The method can be varied to suit almost any river if you know how to fish it properly.

43. Do I think salmon are gut-shy? I don't think so, but of course if the sun makes the cast throw a shadow the finer the cast the better. As an experiment I have tied a big fly to the end of my reel line and caught a fish without any gut at all. That does not look as if they minded gut much. However, in fine, hot weather I think the cast should be fine because the fish may be distracted by the thick gut. I don't think he would be really afraid of it, but it would distract his attention from the fly. It is all a question of proportion : thick gut would not draw a fish's eye away from a *big* fly, but it certainly would from a small one. I hope you see the point I am trying to make. If you are fishing small hooks, you must fish the finest cast so as to make the fly stand out clear of the cast and be noticed by the fish, in preference to the cast. Remember that my flies are very thin, and thick gut would catch the eye of the fish and so he would not notice the fly at all.

Miscellaneous

44. About the sight of fish. This is an unknown quantity; but from watching them I do not think they lose sight of a fly or anything else when they are out of the water. At all events they appear to see enough to avoid colliding with anything, unless they are badly scared. I have caught many a fish making a head and tail rise, and he has taken the fly as he went back into the water; also I have often had them jump a yard and take the fly as they enter the water while the whole of their bodies were still in the air. Therefore I don't think that a fish ever loses sight of his surroundings any more than we should, and I think that their eyesight is better than ours. The water is their element and their judgment of the speed of the fly and of currents is marvellous, so it is an exception for them to miss anything that they go for, unless the fisherman does something that makes the fly act unnaturally. Leave the fly alone as much as possible and let any movement it makes be as natural as possible. Sometimes a fish makes a head and tail rise without opening his mouth, and brings his chin down on the fly; with the idea of drowning it, I suppose. When a fish takes the fly he really sucks it into his mouth by opening his mouth and gills; he does not usually bite on it as we would.

45. You say that you think these big floods will clear the kelts out; but I have never found that

floods made any difference to them. If they are driven down by floods they often work their way up again. Marked kelts have been found miles above the place where they were caught and labelled. My experience of kelts is that they do not go down until their own time, and then only if the temperature suits. Usually they go down on a very small rise of water; six inches or a foot is enough to put the lot out if they are ready to go. They then go in thousands; but I have never seen big floods make any difference to them, except the cock fish which are so weak that they are driven against trees, bushes and rocks, and remain there until they die.

46. About the gums of salmon growing over the teeth. No: I do not think that they do. As far as we have examined there is no indication of this happening, but there is every sign of new teeth forming. Neither can I agree that salmon lose their teeth in fresh water. At present, all the evidence shows that the fish change their teeth at different times, and not necessarily while in fresh water. There is a lot of work to be done in this way yet; but there is no question but that fish in fresh water, and also when they come in from the sea, have teeth that are loose and easily lost, while in kelts the teeth are firm; but we have cases where kelts appear to change their teeth, so it is no use at present saying any more.

I had leave to take kelts for research work and I send the jaws to Dr. Rushton as well as some from fresh fish. During the spring months it is not often that fresh fish have lost their teeth, they are only becoming loose. Autumn fish show more sign of loss of teeth, although occasionally we get some in " full plumage " of teeth, which rather upsets one's ideas of their losing teeth in fresh water.

47. Naturally, Mr. Wood's opinion on the age-long question, " do salmon feed in fresh water "—how many fishing friendships must have been dissolved over the matter! Why do some people get so terribly heated over it?—was sought for. Here is his reply:

A great friend of mine on the Wye has told me that he has often seen salmon feeding on the small fry, and that they dashed about just like pike, and then went back to their lies, although he did not see them actually catch any of the fry. As to worms, I believe it is common knowledge that salmon do not immediately swallow them, but chew them thoroughly, sometimes ejecting them, and taking them in again.

Regarding natural flies ; the salmon take the small gnats and other bigger flies and chew them, or only suck the juices. All I have to go on is the number of times I have seen salmon feeding on fly and invariably finding juices from the vent, which, without much thought, one has put down to what they have been feeding on.

Ever since I have watched salmon I have been convinced that they will take anything on the chance of its being something to eat. I don't, of course, mean that they *always* go for anything that passes them, but at times they will, as everyone knows. I do not think that a salmon has to eat to live while he is in fresh water—he had done all his eating while in the sea.

I am of the opinion that there is no reason to think that salmon do not take solid food in the sea, as they would never get as fat as they do on juices only or make the growth that they do. I should imagine that on the Wye, where small fish are numerous, a certain number of salmon would sometimes take one, perhaps freely, but on the whole I think salmon take the fly and worm and other things just to chew them.

48. About colour-blindness. I do not know why anyone should think that fish are colour-blind. Possibly they may not see colours as we do, and I do not think that colour has much effect upon them, except just a dark or a light one as a contrast.

49. Regarding sound. I think fish feel sound like a good many other animals, and I certainly think that fish have a means of communicating with each other. As to audible sounds, they certainly make them when out of the water, but could they possibly make them when *in* the water where they have not got the air and the combination of mouth and throat

movement? I believe that fish possess additional senses which human beings have lost. As a race, I should say that men have lost more senses than they have gained. In prehistoric times, unless we had more senses than we have now, the entire race would have been wiped out.

50. In answer to your query: I find that the very short, dumpy little fly is taken sometimes, but from experience have concluded that the long, thin fly—and hence the long-shanked hook—are much the best and more freely taken; in fact, much to the surprise of witnesses I have taken sea-trout and salmon freely on a long-shanked hook with the body on, and others on a hook with no body, just a few hairs for the wing and nothing else. This, of course, in summer weather and clear water.

51. You ask the best way to carry fish. At Cairnton we always wrap the fish, after washing him, in a wet cheese cloth. This is by far the best way because it keeps all the flies off him and also all dirt, etc. Keep the fish out of the sun—under some bracken, or something like that.

52. I do not believe in the " colour flash " theory at all; in my opinion it is simply a case of the fly travelling—accidentally or otherwise—at such an angle that it arouses the curiosity of the stiff fish. No fisherman could make his fly travel in exactly the same way at each cast, and although he may *believe* that a different colour would flash and attract

the fish, my idea is that it is the different way in which the fly is presented.

53. Why do I dress the body and wings of my fly so short compared with the length of the hook? I need a small fly in summer weather, say a No. 12, because the fish will not move at anything larger; but although the fish will take these small flies, they are no good at all for holding a fish—the hooks are so very small, and, the eyes being also small, you have to use very fine gut; too fine. I found that salmon did not seem to mind the long, fine hook in the least, and it gave you a chance to hold the fish, and also to use gut of reasonable strength; so I use the fly as it is—small body and wings on a long hook—and it seems to do the trick very well; both attracts the fish and holds on to him afterwards.

You say also that the dressing seems so very thin and would not show against the light. That is an advantage in fine weather. The more indistinct a fly is the better, so I find. If you have a sort of misty, indistinct fly the fish go for it when they would not touch a fully dressed, rather gaudy one, which looks unnatural.

54. You ask if I find a twelve foot rod strong enough to drive in a big hook. Certainly : I have never found the slightest difficulty even when using the very largest of sunk flies. I never use a bigger rod. After all, it does not require a very big pull to bury a fly hook over the barb if the hook is kept decently sharp.

55. Personally, I never cast double-handed. I have always used a single-handed rod, even when fishing big, sunk fly. It is all a matter of taste, and I do not think it makes the slightest difference whether you use a single or double-handed rod, so long as the rod is not too stiff to use fine gut.

Index to Questions.

1. Direction of sun's rays.
2. Effect of atmospheric temperature upon sport.
3. Effect of frosty night upon sport.
4. Effect of state of the moon upon sport.
5. Best type of weather for good sport.
6. Fishing before and after floods.
7. Fishing in a brown water.
8. Effect of white cloud on sport.
9. Upstream wind.
10. Effect of mist on the fishing.
11. Times at which fish will rise.
12. Minimum water temperature at which to fish the greased line.
13. Why salmon refuse a surface fly when air is colder than water.
14. Lie of fish in cold weather and low water.
15. The shadow cast by the fly.
16. " Potted " salmon.
17. Effect of floods on fish.
18. Lie of fish in Spring.
19. Lie of fish in Summer.
20. Striking sharp-rising fish.
21. Sinking a big fly in fast water.
22. Fish following the sunk fly.
23. Permissible amount of drag.
24. Greased line in narrow waters.

25. Method of fishing narrow streams.
26. Fishing deep, slowly-running rivers.
27. Position of angler in relation to that of the fish.
28. Amount of slack to leave on the water.
29. Fishing in Autumn with greased line.
30. Sinking of long line.
31. Use of two flies.
32. Greased line in a big flood.
33. Greased line in slow water.
34. Fish coming to meet the fly.
35. Trick to stir a stiff fish.
36. Cast and fly floating.
37. How a fish comes to the fly.
38. Pricked fish.
39. Fish playing with the fly.
40. Short rising fish.
41. Fishing a long line.
42. Failure of greased line on certain rivers.
43. Are salmon gut-shy?
44. The sight of salmon.
45. Kelts and floods.
46. Teeth of salmon.
47. Do salmon feed in fresh water?
48. Colour-blindness in fish.
49. Effect of sound on fish.
50. Long, slender flies *v.* thick, short flies.
51. Carrying fish.
52. "Colour flash" of flies.
53. Dressing of greased line flies.
54. Striking with a twelve-foot rod.
55. Single- and double-handed casting.

CHAPTER SIX

SUNK FLY

AS a result of the knowledge of line control obtained through the use of the greased line, Mr. Wood fished his sunk flies rather differently to the average salmon angler. His sunk fly work was, as previously mentioned, confined to high water and a cold atmosphere, or when the water was very dirty, or during a frosty evening in April and May. He never used sunk fly if he could persuade salmon to take a fly fished on the greased line, as naturally he preferred to see his fish rise to the surface, where he could follow the whole process of hooking. Of one thing I feel sure, and that is that the fisherman who has practised the greased line method will, as far as possible, apply greased line principles to his sunk fly work.

There are many situations where mending can be done ; and the dropping down of a sunk fly is quite possible and very effective ; while much can be done to control the sinking of the fly in cold weather by judiciously-placed slack. I have collected much information from Mr. Wood's letters in addition to that imparted to me by word of mouth, so I think the following hints may be regarded as fairly representing Mr. Wood's sunk-fly practice.

Flies

As to the right size of fly. When fishing the Aberdeenshire Dee, I should be controlled by temperature. If the weather is very cold, then I use a very big fly; if warmer, a smaller one, but the sizes would range between 4/o½ and 6/o½ inclusive. The size would also be controlled by the depth of the water and its strength; and I like a hook big enough to help me get down to the bottom. Mid-water fishing is no use.

In shallow water you would hook up on the stones if you used a 6/o½, unless you were fishing very strong water. I therefore go down to size 4/o½ or even 4/o¼ if necessary. As to the colour of the fly, I do not care in the least; in fact, one year I fished with Jock Scott only. Another year I amused myself by fishing Mar Lodge all the time; using Gordon any year if the water is peaty or there is a dirty flood. However, I would fish with any fly that anyone liked to name, and should not mind in the least!

When fishing sunk fly, I never use a smaller hook than 4/o; if I want to use anything smaller, I change to greased line and No. 1. My experience is that no sunk fly smaller than 4/o is worth fishing—No. 1 and greased line will beat them every time; and indeed, my sole reason for using a big fly is to get down on to the stones.

Before using a big fly, and especially a Jock Scott, I always cut a good deal of the dressing off it, and simply use the first fly of the right size which comes to hand. I think this makes fishing easier and less expensive, and for those who find the cost of tackle high I should like to say that I keep careful records of every fly I use and fish I kill, and the result shows that there is no need to trouble about colour.

I start with as big a fly as I can use, according to the depth of water. In actual practice, I usually fish all day with a $4/o\frac{1}{2}$ or $4/o\frac{1}{4}$ and do not change it; but fish the pools fast or slow according to their depth. I do this to get the fly well down. If it is very cold and the fish are hanging on the bottom, I use a big $5/o\frac{1}{2}$ or $6/o\frac{1}{2}$, to save time; but that is rare, as in such cold weather fish are in the deadish water and a $4/o\frac{1}{2}$ will soon get there. Once it is down, you can fish it; and there are dodges for sinking a big hook in the way you cast it and sink it *before* it begins to fish, even in strong water. (Mr. Wood in a letter.)

Presentation

Mr. Wood was a firm believer in the efficacy of the fly in high water, and said:

"I should certainly say from my own experience that the fly is more useful than a spinner in the heavy water of Spring. On all occasions except *thick flood* water, the fly is more successful; but in a thick flood —as distinct from ordinary high water—the spinner will do better because it is weighted and more easily gets among the fish at the bottom, where they are sheltering behind the stones; and that is the only reason why bait is better than fly in any water."

The main idea at which Mr. Wood aimed when fishing the sunk fly was to sink his fly as deep as possible without catching on the stones; and also to allow the fly to drop downstream, where possible. In order to accomplish this he threw a slack line, and thereby allowed his fly to sink before the current pulled the line taut, and, in consequence, raised the fly to a certain height, depending on the strength of the stream. Figure 17 shows a straightforward stream and the method of fishing it. The line is cast so that the principal slackness occurs close to the fly, which thus has a slack line on which to sink. To prevent drag upon the main portion of line, the angler mends it upstream before it has time to sink and be gripped by the current. This mend is repeated as often as possible; care being taken not to pull the slack line near the fly. Once a position has been reached in which further mending is impossible, the rod is held fairly high upstream, and then gradually dropped downstream, yielding to the pull of the line. By these means the fly drops down as much as possible, and so covers more water; besides fishing in an attractive manner— more broadside-on to the fish. Should a fish take, the strike is made sideways downstream and in towards the bank. Where the stream is very strong, it is, of course, impossible to mend more than once;

and it may even be necessary to cast at the orthodox angle downstream. In the latter case, cast a slack line so as to give the fly a chance to sink before the line tightens ; give the cast and line a jerk when

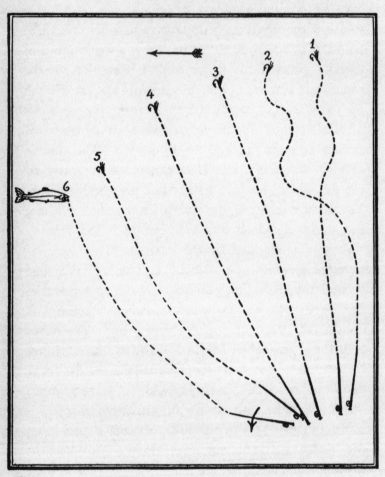

Fig. 17.

Fishing a Sunk Fly. Showing method of sinking fly.

it is on the water and usually the fly will sink well down. The jerk brings the rod well upstream; give way with the point immediately and allow the line to drop downstream, during which process it will usually sink.

As regards the height at which the rod-point should be kept, Mr. Wood said: "I always hold mine within a foot or two of the water, even if I am on a high bank and my rod is pointing straight down as if I were holding a walking stick. Some people have asked me how to hook fish from a high bank and I have always told them to point the rod straight down at the water, so that the tip is about a foot above the surface. By doing this you are giving the same angle to the line and rod as you would if you were wading and held your rod up in the air."

Mr. Wood gave a description of his method when fishing across a stream:

Fishing the far side of the stream I would cast square across with all the slack line in the dead water on the far side of the stream. I would then continue lifting my line upstream the same as with a greased line; not attempting to move or pull the fly in the slack water, but letting it sink. Only when I think it has sunk enough would I let the stream gradually begin to move it; and if I could lift I would continue to do so all the time, but when I expect the fish to take the fly I would be careful not to have any slack line. To hook a fish in deep

water with a big fly and the line slack is almost
an impossibility; if you watch the fish (and on the
Dee the water is sometimes clear enough for you
to see everything) you will see he takes it into his
mouth and spits it out fairly quickly directly he
feels the big, hard hook; but if you have enough
tension on the line to just move the fly—a slight

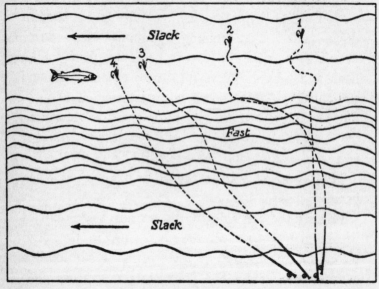

Fig. 18.

Fishing Sunk Fly across a fast run.

tension will cause the stream to move the fly—you
would then have a good chance of hooking the
fish at the back of the mouth as he tries to let go.
I endeavour to keep in touch with a big, sunk fly
all the time (Mr. Wood).

Dead Water

Fishing with big fly and sunk line in dead water I get out as long a cast as I can, wait until I think the fly is nearly on the bottom and then start reeling in rather jerkily, but slowly. I do not jerk or move the rod-point in any way ; and I always keep the rod at an angle with the line so as to avoid a break. Fish are difficult to hook when you are doing this, especially with a very big fly, but for some reason they always come at it. They appear to follow the fly, snap it and turn directly they touch it ; and the reason one does not always hook them is that one has tension on the line and therefore it is pulled straight out of their mouths (Mr. Wood).

Pulling the Fly

I do very little of this ; that is, I very rarely pull the fly but only just keep it moving. If there is not quite enough stream to keep it moving, I try to keep the fly as near the bottom as I can without actually touching and hanging up, but that is all. If one does pull the fly, the most telling way is to let the fly down, and then pull it over the fish from his tail to his head and, as it passes, he will not let it go far in front of him before he goes for it—if he means to have it at all (Mr. Wood).

Covering a Fish behind a Rock

The best way is to make a cast above and just beyond the stone, and let the fly sink. A good deal

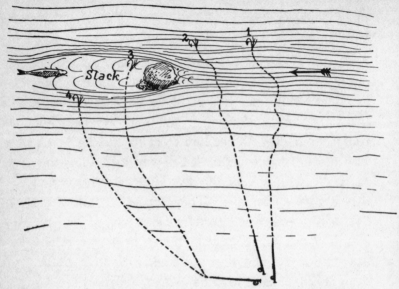

Fig. 19.
Fishing eddy behind a rock with Sunk Fly submerged.

depends upon how high the rock stands in the
water; but if it is a foot below the surface you
can safely let your line sink and drift over it. The
fly will now be sunk deep, and if you bring the
point of your rod round over the bank, or if you
prefer, pull in your line by hand, the fly will straighten
out and be brought square to the fish's eye on the
far side. If you hold your rod over the bank it will
drift diagonally across in front of him (Mr. Wood).

Fishing the Nearer Edge of a Stream

If you are fishing in any strong stream, it is better
to start by casting square across with a short line

into the middle of the stream—or even higher up-stream than square—and let the big fly sink. By the time it has gone down to the usual fishing angle it will be deep, and going deeper. Follow the line with the rod if the slack water moves any line at all, otherwise keep the point of the rod upstream, and let the fly sink and float downstream and into the slack water. I do not mind betting you will have a fish take the fly just as it comes out of the slack water (Mr. Wood).

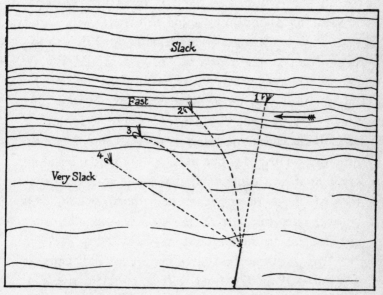

Fig. 20.

Fishing the edge of a fast run with Sunk Fly.

Freeing a Snagged Fly

If by chance I do hook a rock, and as I strike quickly whenever I *feel* anything while I am fishing a sunk fly, I generally get a good hold of it. My next movement to clear it is to pay out a little line, or slacken back ; wait a second or so and then give the line a sharp jerk ; the chances are that the fly has unhooked itself and sunk a little, then a sharp jerk clears the stone. With a short rod and a long line I have little chance of doing what so many do —switch the line over, but I find my method clears the line as a rule. Remember to sharpen the point of the hook before making the next cast (Mr. Wood).

Speaking of sunk fly fishing in general Mr. Wood said : " When you are trying to sink your fly, casting at unorthodox angles and so on, you should always, before you cast, think out the course of the fly. By this I mean you must think whether, by the time the fly has reached the fish, it will be dragging or not. The whole question is almost impossible to describe on paper ; but as a rough guide I should say that if you cannot mend the line it is far better to cast more downstream and more slackly. Of course, once the current *does* grip a sunk line there are no half-measures about it—away goes the fly !

" As regards the location of fish : it certainly depends a good deal on the river, but as to spate rivers or snow-fed rivers—or any river for that matter—the fisherman who is a waterman should know at a glance, or with very little experience, where to fish and how to fish. In cold weather in Spring, salmon lie in the dead water and near the bottom, but never

Plate 10

A CAIRNTON SALMON.

SHOWING HOW A FISH SHOULD BE HOOKED ON THE GREASED LINE IF PROPERLY FISHED.

Plates 11—12

Top : "IN HIM!"

Bottom : THE GHILLIE SHOULD BE KEPT OUT OF SIGHT.

in very streamy water; but they are by no means
glued there, and on a sunny day or one with a warm
air they will take more freely on the surface of the
water than they will if you put on a big fly and fish
the bottom. In the Spring and cold weather, or as
long as the water is cold, they will be in the deepest
and *quietest* water. As it warms up they draw into
the deepest of the *streamy* water, and gradually, as
the river becomes warm, they get into more streamy
and shallow water.

" When snow water is coming down the river you
cannot get a fish except in what we call ' dead
pools,' or dead water, that is, outside the stream in
dead holes with hardly a move in the water. If I
wanted to win some money off a man under those
conditions I would give him a stream to fish and
I would back myself to catch ten to one of his fish;
but I certainly should not fish in a stream or anywhere near it."

Fishable Flood Water

My observations and fishing in fishable floods
lead me to say fish lie in all usual places, mid-stream
or at the side; but in fishable floods you get more
fish at the side because, at the full length of your
cast in mid-stream, you cannot hold and fish a fly
as you should do to enable the fish to come up and
take it. If you could, and sometimes manage to,
you get the fish, and I can do so better with a greased

line; and therefore with this method get as many fish as other people, a great many of them out in the stream.

Incidentally, some people are very afraid of making a noise or vibration in the water, and many of them have argued with me about it. I do not think for a moment from my experience in shallow water amongst fish that either noise or vibration disturb them; all it does is to distract their attention from the fly, and I have never seen a fish quit his lie from the effects of noise.

To go to extremes, we had two years of blasting on the top of my water when they were making the waterworks intake, and we all thought it would spoil those pools; instead of that we found the salmon took quite well after a big blast. The actual blasting took place in a deep channel cut within four or five yards of the bank of the river; and at each blast stones fell like a bursting shell into the pool. Of course, each time they intended to blast they warned us and we had to move into safety, but on returning we invariably got fish! Salmon are funny brutes!

The present chapter, being devoted to the manipulation of sunk lures, perhaps affords as good an opportunity as the whole volume will give for inserting Mr. Wood's views on bait fishing. Although himself a fly-only fisherman, he did not object to others using a bait; far from it:

" I never allow any bait fishing on my water

because it is such good fly water; but I like to watch others bait fishing, although I do none of it myself. On a day when the fish are stiff, if I see anyone baiting in any shape or form I will leave my water to go and fish his pool directly he has finished. I like to see him wade down the middle and splash my side. I have done this, and have had more fish than I care to mention; the bait seems to stir them up and then they go for the fly. I am not against anyone baiting in reason and have found it helpful to me, but not to the baiters. I honestly believe that flies, if used in proper sizes, will beat any sort of bait on any day, except thick mud, and then only because the unleaded fly does not sink deep enough.

"As I said, I like to watch bait fishing, to talk or read about it—for I am interested in *any* method of salmon fishing—but I stick to the fly because I believe it to be the best method.

"While I am on this point of bait stirring up the fish, I should like to say that, in reference to sunk-fly, I do not think there is much in the old theory that 'the first time down the pool is the best.' To my mind, the second time down is likely to be the best if you fail the first, as you have disturbed the fish to a certain extent and they are more awake. Again, your fly may be the proper size this second time; and, by the way, if you stone a pool or swim a dog over it when fish are stiff you will very likely get a salmon immediately afterwards."

CHAPTER SEVEN

THE "WOOD" & "CROSFIELD"
METHODS COMPARED

TO remind the reader of the position which the late Mr. Ernest Crosfield occupied in the world of salmon angling is unnecessary, for he was one of the foremost fishermen of his day. For many years he had paid special attention to the problem of catching salmon under summer conditions, and had evolved a method which came to be known by his own name. Subsequently he wrote an article in *Fisherman's Pie* setting out the chief points which he considered essential to success.

Briefly, he aimed at fishing his fly close to the surface, and to accomplish this he pulled in line by hand, thus never allowing the fly to sink. It will be apparent, therefore, that he was unwittingly pursuing the same road as that taken by Mr. Wood; both endeavoured to fish a fly almost on the surface. After this, their paths diverged; Mr. Wood fished his fly very slowly, Mr. Crosfield very fast; Mr. Wood used the light single hook, Mr. Crosfield the double.

Eventually these two very great anglers became acquainted, with the result that Mr. Crosfield became a convert to the greased line. The story of his conversion is full of interest, and, seeing that Mr. Crosfield was so great a fisherman, should serve to convince any of my readers whose doubts as to the efficacy of the greased line are not yet laid to rest.

Mr. Crosfield had fished the Dee, and often stood opposite Mr. Wood while the latter was fishing. For a long time he had noticed Mr. Wood's arm swing round as he " mended " the line, and wondered— in his own words—" what that man was up to." The next stage was a correspondence which ultimately ripened into personal friendship. The following letters contain, in my view, some of the most valuable information upon the subject of hooking salmon that has ever appeared in print, coming as it does from two of the best fishermen of their day.

First came a discussion upon the merits of flies :

Mr. Crosfield writes :

" I would like you to try the Spotted Dog and Gold and Red *after* you have used one of your sober patterns just to tell us if they will regularly wipe the eye of plain patterns as they do here (on the Wye) though I think it more than possible that this dirty water of the Wye may have something to do with their success here. The point you mention as to these flies having double hooks, and will a salmon spit out a double hook more readily than a single, is interesting. Undoubtedly a trout would, but my experience of salmon is that it makes no difference. Perhaps I have never given as much time as you do, as I never actually give time, but always when possible I allow the fish completely to turn away or go right down without letting it feel any resistance, and if the rod is held at such an angle as permits it being done I ' give the rod.'

"You have carried this summer fishing game into quite a new plane of which I know nothing, but I am more interested than I can tell you. We get something like it on the Helmsdale by using a very short line fished at a right angle and the rod held high and back, and in this way we are able to fish the fly just not cutting. You have gone far beyond this as your plan keeps the fly only just under the surface with any length of line. It is quite certain that you have nothing to learn from me and I everything from you.

"I am in absolute agreement with you about particular shades of colour being just so much nonsense, but I do like to have a dark fly and also a light one."

Mr. Wood's views were :

"Except for a fly out of the ordinary just for an experiment I see no object in changing unless you can convince me that fish are particular as to certain colours. I should be quite happy with one fly only— in various sizes ; in fact, if I started all over again I should use just Black Doctor and Silver Doctor— the one dark and the other light. When I say this I am thinking perhaps more of using big fly, that is sunk fly as if using a bait. We have had a good deal of it this year ; the water being coloured, etc. I then prefer a solid fly, solid wing, but I certainly agree that when fishing a No. 1 or smaller I do prefer a broken wing, in fact almost a hackle fly, and although my Blue Charms have a solid wing, it does not remain so very long as the lightly dressed ones break up in the water. I notice that I catch more fish with old flies than with new ones.

" My chief flies when the water is big and cold are Jock Scott and Mar Lodge. The Jock I put on when the water is coloured and thick, as it is showy, and Mar Lodge when the water is clear, but I don't use these big flies if I can help it."

From flies the discussion moved on to procedure; and Mr. Crosfield said :

" My difficulty is to draw a comparison between your methods and mine because although I have known for years that when small fly fishing the nearer the fly is to the surface the better the result, I suppose that now, knowing your method it should have been obvious that a greased line was the one way to do it. Most of my small fly fishing has been done on the Helmsdale where a *very* short line cast square with the water could be kept as near the surface as desired by rod management, but here is where your method differs so greatly—with the greased line you can work the fly slowly and near the surface, but with the other style the fly must be worked quite fast or, of course, it goes deep. Anyway, I hadn't the brains to tumble to grease !

" I also have caught many fish casting more square (upstream) but have always had the idea—evidently from your letter quite wrong—that salmon would not take a fly if it drifted down on its own, i.e., it must have motive power to show that it was a living thing, so I have always 'pulled through' quite fast in order to make the fly work across as well as down, indeed I do this when casting square or anywhere nearly square across stream. It really seems as if the greatest difference between your method and ordinary good fishing is a question of pace. I have always fancied that in low, clear water summer fishing, more fish are caught by working the fly as fast as possible, so as not to let them have time to see too much and to make them dash at it. This is entirely exploded by your method and the amazing results.

" The question I asked you about letting the fly go downstream was not clear, I meant *straight* down after it has come to the right spot. Take a place on the Helmsdale I know. On a straight, plain stream about twenty-five feet across and four to five feet deep, all gravel, with a fifteen feet rod you stand with your toes touching the water, cast square to just reach the backwater across the stream, hold the rod square and *still* and when the fly comes round and hangs at right angles to the rod, very slowly give way with the rod and up he comes. There are three spots on the Helmsdale where they absolutely won't rise at you at all unless you drop the fly down to them like that.

" I feel that I have to begin over again and everything to learn! I can't even imagine your thinking that you have not made a good cast if you feel the line pull the rod. This shows the absolute difference between my method and greased line, for I have never felt as if I was fishing unless I felt in absolute touch with the fly, but in one particular I don't like being in this immediate touch, you feel the fish too soon and it hasn't time to turn round before it feels the hook."

Mr. Wood replied :

" I remember in your article in Farlow's Catalogue you said that to make a fish take, the small fly had to be drawn quickly over him. Your comments on the greased line clearly answer this point, as you know now that I work the fly slowly—just the opposite to you, and this evidently makes *all* the difference.

" Now as to a salmon not taking a fly if it floated down on its own I should like to repeat Colonel Mainwaring's remark when he saw me fishing—' You seem to let your fly float down like a dead thing.' I agreed, but you must not forget that although it is floating downstream there are always little eddies which move the fly an inch or two in any direction. In the majority of the pools I find I do the same with small fly on the surface or big fly sunk deep, and I find it is more killing than if worked in the orthodox way. I have found that a fly drifting down stream and very slightly across is the most effective. You, in that pool on the Helmsdale, clearly proved that practically the only way to get a fish was to let the fly drop down to them. Now was it end on or partly sideways so that they had a clear view of it? Both for hooking and making a fish take, I find it much more effective to give them a more or less side view of the fly.

" With regard to your remark about making the fish dash at the fly. I have found that when fooling about with the fish, trying tricks and standing in the water amongst them, I have held a fly over a fish practically stationary or moving so slowly that he had plenty of time to look at it and swim round it. They appear to take no notice, but all of a sudden they make up their minds to have it. Then they come up quickly and very quietly, take it as if nothing on earth mattered—so slowly that you dare not strike or do anything, just let the current tighten the line downstream by dropping the point of the rod. In a few seconds you know whether he has the fly, and in a few seconds more you know if the fish is hooked or not. Dropping the rod-point of course, makes the line tighten from downstream and pulls the fly into the corner of the mouth.

" Regarding what I said about not liking to feel the line, I find that this applies when fishing with heavy fly and sunk line. It applies to the extent that I find I am fishing better and making a surer job of holding my fish if I do not feel a drag on the line. The same certainly applies to greased line where the less weight on the rod the better. Of course, there are places where you must be in touch with the fly and a slack line would not pay, but these are not many. I wonder where you keep your rod-point. With big sunk fly and line I keep the point about a foot above the water.

" There is a lady up here who seems to beat all the men. In watching her fishing with big fly she appears to cast well downstream and let the fly come slowly round, keeping the rod-point what I should call high, say four to six feet. I cast very much more square across the stream and let the fly come round slowly, keeping the point of the rod low, so what is there in it ?

" I tried your double hook and I cannot say I like it, for this reason—that I should, I think, have to alter my method of fishing. The few fish that have so far taken hold of the double hook seem to let go *immediately*, as no doubt when they shut their mouths they feel something solid which they cannot squash. With my small, light flies on single hook, when they shut their mouths they seem to continue to hold the fly and chew it, so I have plenty of time before I tighten, but not so with your doubles.

" Now about the straight line and the amount of slack or bag for the fish to turn before feeling the pull—it is all a matter of watching the line and the currents, as I said before, you have to put the loose line into the proper place."

Mr. Crosfield in reply :

" You have solved the double *v.* single hook matter for your style of fishing. There were only two points in question, the first vital : Will the fish take the double as well as the single, and if so does the double reduce the percentage of losses ? Having decided the first in the negative there is nothing further to consider, I had no chance of proving this one way or the other, as, fishing fast in the ordinary way and being in immediate contact with the fly I, of course, tightened as soon as I felt anything. It is amazing that you can leave the fish as long as you do —leave them to do just as they like with the fly, and then after all to find them hooked when you tighten.

" The Wye here, I fear, will never lend itself to floating line ; never enough fish, never really clear water and the fish in deeper water than 80 per cent. or 90 per cent. of what you fish, though, I have one place that is likely looking and shall be tried."

Mr. Wood to Mr. Crosfield :

" What a year we are having. The water has been so very high all this spring. I find this high water a very different game, and it is difficult to hang a fly over a fish. I expect I should do better if I used a twenty-foot rod as there are only a few places where —in this strong water—I can hang the fly at all. This will interest you—I find that if I can see a fish acting like a porpoise, somewhere near the bank or near a jetty I can make a bet that I will get him. So

far, I have had them every time. The way I go for
the fish is with a short line about a yard longer than
the rod, get close to the fish and dap for him. It is
most amusing to see a fish come for the fly quite slowly
on the surface, sometimes with his head out of the
water. Of course, as soon as he takes you have to
place your line on the water in the direction from
which he comes, by dropping the point of the rod.
You can see the expression on the fish's face, eyes,
spots and everything else !

" I got into difficulties with one fish, but got him
all right, as he took the fly within six feet of me
as I stood in the water. He must have been somewhere
near my feet as he appeared to come from in front
and across me. What I should like to know is what
Francis Ward would say about how far a salmon can
see a fly, as the distance they seem to see a dapped fly
skimmed on the surface seems to me to be beyond what
Ward states, and they must be able to see very clearly
as they make no bones about it. I got seven last week
in this way. Salmon don't seem to be frightened of
the fisherman, at least they don't mind my ' bulk ' ! "

Mr. Crosfield :

" It wasn't difficult to picture all you describe in
low clear water but when you can beat everyone else
in heavy high water it is much more difficult. When
you talk of hooking in the part of the mouth you
wish to you must be approaching complete perfection.
I think that in the ordinary way when I get a good rise

that shows really well that I unconsciously stop the rod to give the fish time to turn to at least broadside before he feels me or I feel him, this is with the hope that he may be hooked in the corner of the mouth, which I have found the best of all holds. The fish that I lose the highest percentage of are those that take straight (or nearly straight) downstream from me, fish which take the fly like a feeding chalk stream trout, which simply lift straight up and quietly sink again but do *not* turn. Lazy autumn fish favour this way of rising. I expect with your slow method of fishing many fish take in this way and that is why you find it pays so well to place the line on the water in the direction from which he came; as he would probably return the same way he came he would give you the chance of hooking in the way you desire.

"It is wonderful to me that you can make a certainty of getting those porpoise-like fish, for personally I have always found them most difficult to catch.

"I emphatically disagree with Francis Ward and his 'angle of vision,' 'fish's window,' and so on. I have had many examples of both salmon and trout seeing at a very wide angle, and I doubt there being any angle at which they cannot see both under water, on the surface and above the water, so I am afraid that I cannot accept what he says.

"One thing that would be most interesting to prove and which I think you could probably decide is whether fish (salmon in particular) taste or smell anything (food) in the water. Though it may be against all your principles I do wish you would get a bottle containing the glycerine in which prawns have been preserved, dip your fly in it, and before all the glycerine and smell has washed off put it in front of a fish and see if he chews it even better for the savoury ! ! ! wash."

Mr. Wood in reply :

" We ended the Spring season with 449 for three rods, and the water has been at flood height the whole Spring. In May the height averaged 3 ft. 8 ins., and as our best fishing height for May is about 1 foot you will see what a poor chance we had for using fine tackle, but for all that I got 244 fish myself out of our total of 449 and as I have been feeling a bit seedy this Spring I have had to take things easier than I generally do. This loafing gave me a chance to watch some of my friends fishing. I wanted to see why I caught more fish than they did, as after all I am only a beginner compared with most of them.

" I was immediately struck by their extraordinary lack of attention to the fly and its position as it was fishing after they had made the cast. It was an eye-opener to me to see some of the old hands on the Dee casting. To my mind some of the casting could not be worse, for they did not seem to trouble where the fly fell. I clearly saw that my success in

the high water has been entirely due to care in the
matter of casting and controlling the line.

"This year when fishing with the big sunk flies
so many of them said that they could not touch a
fish. I asked them if they ever experienced little
pulls from trout, and they all said that they had;
so then I asked if the pulls occurred just half way
round in the drift or immediately below where
they were standing. The answer again was yes. I
then told them that I believed that all these little
pulls were given by salmon. Of course they refused
to believe it; but I asked them to strike at each
pull in future and to strike in towards the bank;
or, better still, to watch the line just where it entered
the water and at the slightest movement give a
quick, sharp strike. The result was that most of
them began to get fish! Personally, this year I
began by feeling these little pulls which I also thought
were trout and paid no attention, but I soon discovered I was wrong. Now I feel sure that the
fish came for the big fly near the bottom, and came
upstream at speed taking the fly with them and
letting go immediately they felt the hard hook.
What one really felt was the sudden greater pull of
the water on the bellied line, so in certain positions
of the cast I began to look out for these pulls and
by striking very quickly hooked the fish.

"Fishing small fly in the strong water I often found
fish taking in the same way, without seeing them,

but of course on light gear one feels the little pull (of the stream) very much sooner, and with the No. 1 hook they do not let go so quickly.

"I am glad you agree with me concerning Francis Ward and the fish's window. In my experience I have yet to discover what the fish *cannot* see. I *have* discovered what they *can* see and that appears to be everything.

"Why has not someone written a chapter on 'Hooking the Salmon?' Someone should write on 'Hooking a fish where you want to!' The whole thing comes back to the speed and angle of the fly when the fish takes it.

"I had no chance of giving your prawn-glycerine a trial, but personally I think all fish have a great sense of smell and that salmon have it also; but I think a salmon takes a fly to be the natural insect, and therefore does not bother much about the smell."

Mr. Crosfield to Mr. Wood :

"I am not at all surprised at your amazement concerning the lack of attention shown by nineteen fishermen out of twenty, for I have so seldom seen anyone really concentrate and keep in immediate touch (old style) with their fly; and by touch I mean quite as much watching it carefully as by feeling. The line is chucked out at any angle and allowed to swim round as it likes while the man with the rod is admiring the view, or talking to his ghillie, while many of them swag the rod about so that they could not even feel their fly. I have enough fishing faults, I know, but not want of concentration. Possibly for this reason I have (I think) fewer losses and hook more rising fish than does the casual fisher. It has always seemed to me that some men hook and land more fish than others and I have always put this down to their automatically tightening on their rises—a kind of instinct; but from what you say it is probably superior watchfulness, or rather, extra concentration.

" I agree with you as to the desirability of hooking a fish in the corner of the mouth as this part is tougher than any other and offers a sure hold for a small hook.

" Last year here we had a quite exceptionally low river in March and April, and some slack water opposite my house, averaging nine to ten feet, was full of kelts. I have never moved a clean fish there so I thought it would be interesting to try if the kelts would take a 1/o Caroline. Not wishing to hook them I kept two or three yards of slack line in my hand; they rose freely and were allowed to swim away with the fly and *all the slack* to avoid the trouble of hooking and landing them, but to my surprise this was the best way to defeat my object; the more slack given and therefore the longer before tightening, the better were they hooked, and practically all of them in the corner of the mouth. Not one of them rejected the fly. The water was very clear and every rise easily visible so that I could see everything that happened.

"I don't think I get those touches from trout— at least, I don't think that they come from trout; but of course I have experienced thousands of those indescribable little plucks from salmon, and especially from those quick, shy surface rises. How they do it is a mystery. Is it just the edge of the lips, or a touch with the body?

"The touch which we call a knock when bait-fishing is very frequent, one can feel a leap if the fish is touched by the bait; and when a fish comes with a rush from more or less behind the bait it 'hits' it and I suppose is carried past it by its impetus and there is quite an appreciable moment between the knock and the real pull.

"I should be extremely interested to see you fish strong water with rod held up and loose line in your hand ready to give slack. The fish that rise straight below you and fall straight back *without turning*, have always been the most difficult to hook; but I never heard of a remedy until you wrote to me about your method. Probably no one has written about hooking the fish, because nothing is known about it; but now you really seem to have solved the great problem, for I feel sure that you are right."

Time has proved that Mr. Wood was entirely correct; nowadays the greased-line fisherman speculates not as to whether he will hook the fish, but where he will hook him. What an advance in technique !

The correspondence shows that Mr. Crosfield had trembled upon the verge—as one might say—of making the discovery which Mr. Wood actually made. His angle of approach was different, but he had achieved the same result by other means except in the important matter of hooking fish. Here Mr. Wood stood alone. It must be remembered that these two very great anglers had each killed many hundreds of fish, and no finer testimony to the efficacy of Mr. Wood's methods can be offered than that Mr. Crosfield, with all his successes and experience behind him, should unhesitatingly endorse the greased line as the method of the future. The value of his letters lies, to my mind, in the fact that here we have the more or less orthodox point of view confronted with startling and revolutionary discoveries ; here we have the very man equipped with the necessary experience which would enable him to assess the value of this (then) new idea. And with what results ? He immediately realises the full value of this method. I recollect a friend saying : " If Crosfield says so then I for one am not going to argue the point." This remark related to another fishing matter ; but I sincerely hope that any doubting Thomas will follow my friend's example and accept the testimony of the expert witness in this case.

CHAPTER EIGHT

THE CAIRNTON RECORDS

MR. WOOD has given a very good description of the water and conditions at Cairnton, and I do not think I can do better than quote his letters on this subject :

" Regarding the Aberdeenshire Dee as a whole, I should think a fair estimate would be about eleven thousand fish killed in an average good year; but owing to there being so many short beats and no figures actually published, it can only be an estimate ; but I think for our best years this figure is on the small side.

" Our legal season is for nine months, but my beat may be taken as being fairly representative of others on the river, and is about the lowest of the middle ones. Whatever the weather, hot or cold, on the opening day the pools are stocked with fish, so that we begin to get fish on the 11th February ; but all my fishing is over by the end of May or first week in June, so the season can be called four months only.

" The lower beats are not good unless there is very hard weather, when the fish enter the river and remain for some time in the lower water ; but if the weather is warm they run through and stop in the middle beats, so that the lower waters as a rule have not a great deal of fish, and all their fishing is over by May.

"The middle beats would be the same as myself from the opening up to the middle of June, after that not good; but the upper beats begin to get good fishing whatever the water by the first of April. They have increasingly good fishing up till the middle of July, after that, as a rule, all fishing is over for the rest of the year except for a few odd fish caught by people who take the shootings, but, of course, these fish are all red by then.

"In the Autumn there is sometimes a small run of fish in September or early October, but it is very rare that they get as high up the river as my beat before the season closes. A few of the lower beats get just a few fish, so, although our season is in theory a long one, in practice it really amounts to about four months, and the majority, if not all the fish, are caught during those months.

"The river is owned by so many people, most of whom let their fishing, that it is all split up into small beats of from half a mile to a mile or two, and I should say on the average there would be two rods on each bank for every mile of water, often more.

"The Dee fish seem to start running into the river in December, and we could well open in January, I think; but at present the law says the 11th of February. I think the fish are gradually coming up earlier, and it is possible that the opening day may be altered to suit at some future date. The fish continue entering the river in small shoals from December until the end of May, and after that very few come in; just little driblets. Some years there is a small run of grilse in June and the beginning of July, and also some sea trout.

"The water temperature in July and August often touches 70°F., but as there are no fresh fish and only red potted ones no one tries for them except occasionally an odd rod and a few local people, and I think they get most of their fish on worm.

"As regards enemies to the salmon, we have sharks, porpoises, seals, saithe, coal fish and congers, the latter playing havoc among the smolts. It has been proved that coal fish hang about the mouth of the rivers when smolts are emerging into the shallow water, and have been caught full of smolts. There are three authentic records of sharks caught in the North Sea when one had ten salmon, and the other eight salmon, three cod fish and one saithe, in their stomachs. Also, another shark caught quite close to Aberdeen had three salmon in it.

"We also have a lot of Merganser, Goosander, and Black-headed gulls and terns, all of them living to a great extent on salmon parr and smolts. Trout and eels are certainly bad poachers. Eels probably do not take much spawn since they are hibernating at that time, but they do take salmon fry. There are several records of cases where over two hundred salmon eggs have been taken out of a half-pound brown trout, and they are probably the worst enemies of the salmon in our rivers, while a sea trout is not much better. Young sea trout have been found full of salmon eggs—one kelt sea trout had over four hundred.

"On our (Scottish) coasts there are no restrictions as to nets, as long as they are 400 yards—in most cases —away from the channel at the mouth of the river. Different parts of the coast are let to different people, and it is left to them to place any number of nets they like. On those parts of the coast where there are no rivers, you will see salmon nets every few hundred yards. In many cases, eight bag nets may be seen in line, one behind the other extending half a mile out to sea.

"And now as to the Cairnton figures. I was a sub-tenant starting July, 1913, and consequently I only had the water at different periods up to 1919; i.e., I had to take turn about with the other tenants. After that I became the sole tenant; so the figures of fish caught by me between 1913 and 1919 are for part-time fishing only—after that, for full time.

"My water consists of under two miles of river, and about three-quarters of it is fishable, although not all the pools; but the great majority of the water consists of good pools. In a hard winter I have good sport, as a rule, because the fish go up slowly and rest in my water a good deal. In a mild winter they go through us quickly and rest in the pools above, so the beats above us usually have record takes in years when we do not do so well.

" When I am fishing in the spring I generally limit my water to three rods, but very often only two, depending on the height of the water."

Before giving some selections from the Cairnton figures, I think a few remarks as to the general habits of Dee salmon, as noted by Mr. Wood, might well be inserted.

As to salmon taking natural flies, Mr. Wood says: " If there is a big hatch of March Brown, the feeding instinct of salmon comes out on occasion. I have seen well over a hundred fish feeding at the same time and I could not keep my fly out of their mouths, having got in touch with forty-one that day and landed sixteen. I only wish I had known then what I do now about hooking the fish—that was in 1915 or 1916. Since that time I have seen a number of salmon feeding altogether on March Brown; and on many occasions both kelts and fresh fish taking my March Brown."

Regarding the temperature of the air and the water—" Makes this great difference. If the air is warmer than the water, then fish the surface. Greased line will get more fish than sunk fly at all times of the season. I put the reason down to the immediate

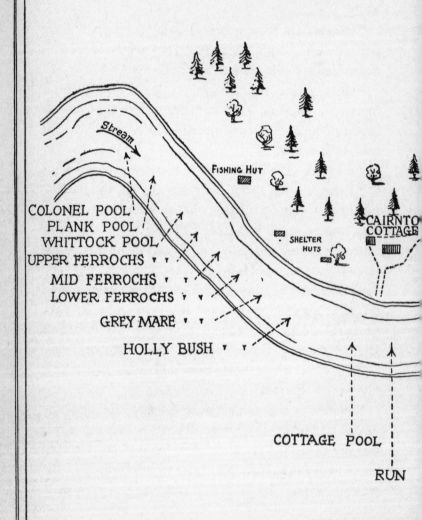

CAIRNTON

Stream

FISHING HUT

COLONEL POOL
PLANK POOL
WHITTOCK POOL
UPPER FERROCHS
MID FERROCHS
LOWER FERROCHS

GREY MARE

HOLLY BUSH

SHELTER
HUTS

CAIRNTO
COTTAGE

COTTAGE POOL

RUN

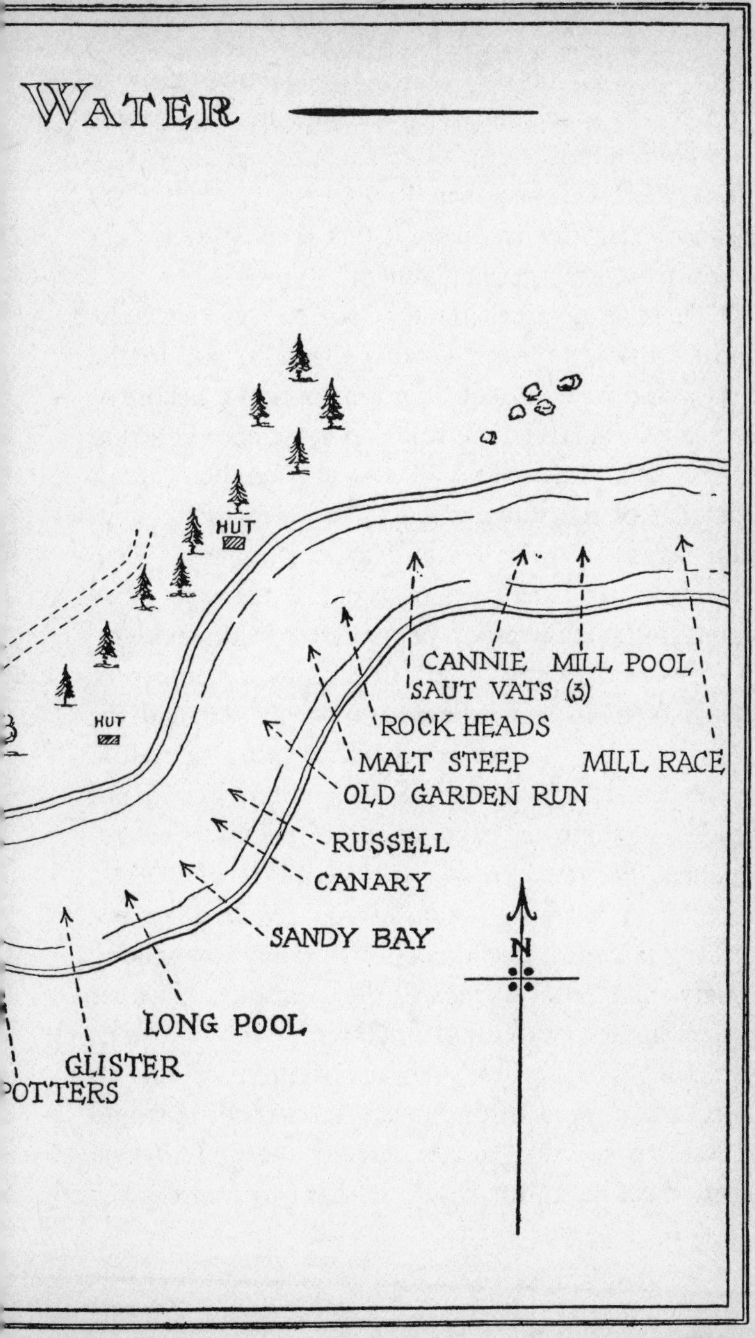

WATER ————

HUT

HUT

CANNIE MILL POOL
SAUT VATS (3)
ROCK HEADS
MALT STEEP   MILL RACE
OLD GARDEN RUN
RUSSELL
CANARY
SANDY BAY

N

LONG POOL

GLISTER
POTTERS

Fig. 21.

effect of the air on the water; the fish like it, and it gives them life just like it does to us. Fish are practically cold-blooded, but air temperature in some way affects them quicker than it does us. I think they are more sensitive in all ways, yet they do not seem to feel pain, only get frightened.

"There is no question that so long as the air is warmer than the water I can get fish to rise to the surface and take my small fly whatever the height of the water. There is one thing to remember and that is, that the temperature of the air can be warmer than that of the water when there is ice about; but there are many evenings in May in the North when the air, even if it feels warm, is colder than the water owing to the temperature of the water being so high; and this is a simple point that quite a number of people seem to miss. Because it is summer and the air is hot they do not think about the temperature of the water, which may be still hotter, but in hot weather in summer the difference of the temperatures need not be great, in fact the air might be slightly colder than the water and still you get fish, but not for long; it soon puts them down. I am now talking of very small flies. As regards the question of whether oxygen in the water has anything to do with the fish rising. Of course, the temperature of the air affects the oxygen in the water, but I think it would be hard to say that that is actually the point which affects the fish, and it would be hard to find out for certain as I get fish on the surface if the sun is out and there is a warmish wind, or none at all, even with blocks of ice floating about. At that time the fish lie in dead water, or nearly so, and not in the stream because they obtain plenty of oxygen without going into the broken water. The opposite, of course, is the case in April and May when air and water temperatures are high. Those who fish sunk fly only say that temperatures make little difference to them ; but in my own case I find they control the height at which I fish."

As to the artificial flies and the reason for salmon taking them. " Why not as food and remembrance of parr days, and the fun of hunting in a sense ? I am sure they take my March Brown for the natural ; and I have seen them take anything once they begin to feed, even leaves and twigs, and in one case a bit of burnt gorse—this fish was caught with the gorse in its gullet. I have always noticed that a hatch of grannom sickens the fish and puts them down, but not so the March Brown. You do get blank days with May Fly or March Browns about, but when there is a big hatch of grannom you get a poor day while it lasts, and often nothing at all. I have never seen them take even one grannom.

" I have often noticed that fish lying in tidal waters, or in pools which the tide may get into on particular occasions—if not every tide—always seem to wake up and make a move at the time the tide should be up. Instinct seems to tell them and they get lively; either they start cruising about or else running up the river, but if the water is not suitable they appear to cruise in circles, and one can very often get them. On one occasion I saw them 'milling.' Personally, I have never caught any when the water has actually been salt, but in brackish water I have had some good fun."

Dee fish do not appear to fear man, and Mr. Wood's experience was that "Salmon have no idea what a man is any more than a cow, and they pay no attention at all to a man as a man; in fact, it takes a lot to frighten fish, and I am speaking now of other rivers I know besides the Dee. If fish are running, walking past them will disturb them and they go off quietly, but if they are resting they will often let you walk within gaffing distance, and you can stand still and look at them. If you know what you are doing and are careful you can tickle salmon the same as brown trout, and the trout certainly is more used to man and most certainly is frightened. Commonsense should tell you that the salmon cannot dislike man, never having seen one, and the few he does see on a river do not disturb or harm him."

Scale Reading

When fishing, Mr. Wood usually carried in his pocket one of those miniature microscopes beloved of scale readers.[1] These little instruments, although of low power, are quite efficient for their purpose. The outer glass at the large end is made to unscrew ; the scale is placed inside and the cap replaced. Thus the scale is held flat against the large lens, and by holding the instrument to the eye and facing the light, it is easy to obtain a quite satisfactory reading—at all events, from the ordinary angler's point of view. The spawning mark and years of sea and river-life can usually be seen quite clearly. See plates 15 and 16, kindly lent by Mr. J. Arthur Hutton. Mr. Wood wrote :

" Those really interested in fishing should carry a small glass to enable them to inspect scales of fish caught. You often see a curiously-marked fish and by reading the scales you very often know the reason why. Also it is very interesting to know that you may have caught a fish that has spawned twice or is up for its second spawning."

He also thought that, if more anglers read scales, there would be a very beneficial increase in our knowledge of the habits of salmon. In many cases, records of scale reading from rivers where it is little practised, would lead to the acquisition of extremely valuable knowledge.

Water height & temperature

Mr. Wood fitted up a water gauge in his fishing lodge at Cairnton, piping the water up from the

[1] These microscopes are priced at approximately 7*s*. 6*d*.

river. The gauge was fitted with maximum and minimum indicators so that the fluctuations of water-level during the night could be ascertained. In addition, he kept very careful records of the water heights and their relation to the number of fish caught.

Temperature readings were taken and recorded, both for the air and the water; and examples of these records are given in the following pages.

Sunday Work

Sunday being a *dies non*, so far as fishing is concerned, Mr. Wood made a practice of overhauling his fishing gear on that day. It says much for his enthusiasm that he regularly dismantled, oiled and cleaned all his reels which were in use; broke all the rod joints in order to prevent any jamming through prolonged engagement, and generally examined all his gear. Regarding jammed rod-joints, he gave a very useful hint: " Slightly warm the joint, but only enough to warm any grease that has been put on the joint, which, of course, should not have been put on. If the bayonet joint holds, and force is needed, two men are better than one and do less harm to the rod. Each person has one hand on each portion of the rod; if my left-hand was the lowest your hand would come next, then the joint, then my right hand, and finally your left facing it.

THE FINISH OF A "MEND."

THE LATE MR. ERNEST CROSFIELD WITH ONE OF
HIS TROPHIES.

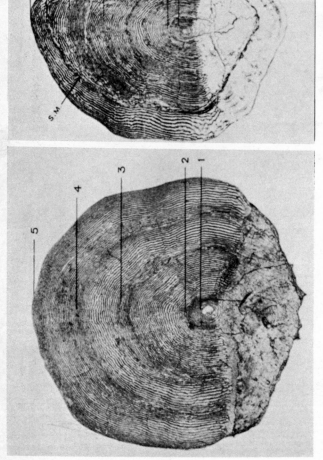

SCALE FROM 34¼-LB. LARGE SPRING FISH.

MALE. LENGTH 45 INCHES, GIRTH 23 INCHES. THIS FISH WAS A MAIDEN OR UNSPAWNED FISH. 2 YEARS' RIVER LIFE, 3 COMPLETE YEARS' FEEDING IN THE SEA.

23¼-LB. SPAWNED FISH.

FEMALE. LENGTH 40 INCHES, GIRTH 21 INCHES. 2 YEARS' RIVER LIFE, RETURNED AS A SMALL SUMMER FISH AFTER SPENDING ABOUT 2½ YEARS FEEDING IN THE SEA AND SPAWNED THAT YEAR. WENT BACK TO THE SEA AS A KELT EARLY IN THE FOLLOWING YEAR AND RETURNED THE NEXT YEAR TO SPAWN FOR THE SECOND TIME.

Plates 15—16

The rod is held very firmly, and the unscrewing motion is much easier.

"In the case of a suction joint that really has stuck; if two men cannot pull it apart with their hands in the positions I have just mentioned, I have found that there is absolutely no trouble at all if two other men hold on to the ends of the rod and slightly pull. Their pulling does almost more than the two in the middle; but this, of course, should be on a very rare occasion."

The first example of records is a summary of the season 1931, which shows how Mr. Wood tabulated his results. In all cases I have omitted the names of his guests as they would probably prefer to remain anonymous. This is a record Cairnton year.

The next example is from the day-to-day record book, and shows the details of fish caught, pools, size and patterns of flies, temperature, height of water and weather, together with incidental notes. I have taken a page from the record year of 1931 as a good example of the daily recording. The two water and temperature readings are those for morning and evening, and the letters N.E. refer, of course, to the direction of the wind.

The next table gives the yearly bags at Cairnton from 1913 to 1934—the year of Mr. Wood's death—and shows catches by all rods and by Mr. Wood himself.

Piscators	Fish	
A. H. E. Wood	202	*Spring Fish*=753
33 other Rods		*Total Weight*=7,398¾ lbs.
(Guests and	551	*Average*=9 lb. 13 oz.
Ghillies) for Spring		
fishing.		No. of fish 20 lb.
		and over =18
		No. of fish 10 lb.
		to 20 lb. =202
		Biggest day's fishing=May 19th
		23 fish
		Biggest Week's fishing=May 18th to 23rd
		108 fish
Total Spring Fish	753	Ten fish or over in a day caught by,
Autumn and		A. H. E. Wood=19th May, 12
Summer Fish	74	Guest=29th April and 30th April, 11 (2)
		Guest=5th May, 10
Total 1931	827	Guest=20th May, 10
		Spring fish of 20 lb. or over caught by,
		A. H. E. Wood (4) 24½, 23¾, 21½, 20
		Guest (3) 25¾, 21, 20¾
		,, (2) 24¾, 20½
		,, (2) 23, 22½
Autumn Fish :		,, (1) 29½
20 lb. or over.		,, (1) 26
(4) 34, 22, 29 20 lb.		,, (1) 22
		,, (1) 22
		,, (1) 21¼
		,, (1) 20¼
		,, (1) 20
		Total=18

Previous Best Totals.

		1931 *Season*
For Day . .	23	23
,, Week . .	87	108
,, Month . .	259	341
,, Spring Fishing	659	753
,, Year . .	707	827

FLIES USED IN SPRING					
	All Rods.	A.H.E.W.		All Rods.	A.H.E.W.
Blue Charm	393	155	*Brought forward*	668	197
Jock Scott	77	22	Beauley	11	5
Akroyd	36		Jeannie	10	
March Brown	33	13	Killer	9	
Brora	32		Dusty Miller	8	
Silver Dr.	30	7	Dallas	7	
Golden Knight	23		Logie	7	
Mar Lodge	17		Gledwing	4	
Silver Blue	16		Torrish	4	
Cairnton	11		Odds	25	
	668	197	Totals	753	202

CAIRNTON SPRING FISHING, 1931
HOURS FISH WERE CAUGHT
By all Rods

1931—Time	8-9	9-10	10-11	11-12	12-1	1-2	2-3	3-4	4-5	5-6	6-7	7-8	8-9	9-10	10-11	11-12	Total
February Fish	—	2	2	7	10	3	4	16	16	7	1	—	—	—	—	—	68
March ,,	—	1	6	9	9	8	4	18	19	16	23	5	—	—	—	—	117
April ,,	—	—	10	17	18	11	9	25	18	8	9	19	13	8	—	—	165
May ,,	1	9	36	50	48	23	10	23	24	26	10	19	23	58	41	2	403
Total	1	11	54	83	85	45	27	82	77	57	43	43	36	66	41	2	753

By A. H. E. Wood

1931—Time	8-9	9-10	10-11	11-12	12-1	1-2	2-3	3-4	4-5	5-6	6-7	7-8	8-9	9-10	10-11	11-12	Total
February Fish	—	—	—	1	5	2	—	4	3	1	—	—	—	—	—	—	16
March ,,	—	—	—	2	2	2	1	3	5	2	10	—	—	—	—	—	27
April ,,	—	—	—	4	7	4	—	2	5	2	2	6	1	2	—	—	35
May ,,	1	2	5	18	15	7	3	7	7	10	5	5	8	22	9	1	124
Total	1	2	5	25	29	15	4	16	20	15	17	11	9	24	9	1	202

Date	Pool	Rod	Salmon & Grilse No.	Salmon & Grilse W'ght.	Fish on	Fly	Size Hook	Time	Trout W'ght.	Trout No.	Remarks
May 19th	Long Pool	A. N. Other	5	9	277	Blue Charm	6	10.35 a.m.			2 ft. 2 ins. 48°. N.E.
	"			6¾	8	"	6	11.25 "			Cold dull day.
	Canary			7	279	"	6	1.0 p.m.			2 ft. 0 ins. 50°. Sun at times. A big lot
	Run of Old Garden			8½	11	March Brown	8	2.45 "			of fish in pools and
	Cottage			7¼	2	Torrish	4	10.30 "			also running.
	Upp. Ferrochs	W. Blank	6	9	280	Blue Charm	7	1.10 "			
	Plank			7¾	1	"	7	3.10 "			
	Grey Mare			12	2	"	4	4.45 "			
	"			10½	3	"	4	5.10 "			
	Cottage			20¾	4	"	4	6.0 "			
	Old Garden			8¼	5	"	4	7.35 "			
	Cottage	A. H. E. Wood	12	7	6	"	6	11.30 a.m.			
	"			15¼	7	"	6	11.55 "			
	"			9¾	8	"	6	12.15 p.m.			
	"			8¼	9	"	6	12.40 "			
	"			9½	290	"	4	1.5 "			
	Grey Mare			10¾	1	"	4	2.15 "			
	"			16¾	2	"	4	2.30 "			
	Upp. Ferroch			14	3	"	6	5.25 "			
	Whittock			11	4	"	6	6.50 "			
	Upp. Ferroch			9	5	"	6	6.55 "			
	Grey Mare			8	6	"	3	10.15 "			2 ft. 48°
	"			8	297	"	3	10.30 "			1 ft. 9 in. 40°. N.
May 20th	Cottage	A. H. E. Wood	5	9	8	"	6	9.15 a.m.			V. cold dull day.
	"			11	9	"	3	11.30 "			Frost at night. Big
	"			9	300	"	6	3.5 p.m.			shoal of fish arrived
	Grey Mare			15¾	1	"	6	5.5 "			lower beat in even-
	Whittock			7¼	2	"	6	8.5 "			ing and reached Grey Mare 10.0.
		C.f.	582	5,698							

			By all Rods	By A. H. E. Wood	
1913	(Autumn only)		28	14	
1914	(Feb. 11th to June 19th)		224	99	
1915	(Feb. 11th to May 11th)		429	265	Mr. Wood took 121 fish in 13 consecutive days.
1916	(Feb. 11th to May 31st)		481	272	
1917	(Feb. 11th to April 30th)		207	133	
1918	(Feb. 11th to April 30th)		193	118	
1919	(June 24th to Oct. 31st)		50	18	Very low water all Summer.
1920	(For whole season)		707	343	
1921	do.	do.	290	152	Warm dry Spring. Fish ran through Cairnton Water.
1922	do.	do.	567	286	
1923	do.	do.	605	311	
1924	do.	do.	391	190	
1925	do.	do.	479	244	
1926	do.	do.	505	239	
1927	do.	do.	520	158	
1928	do.	do.	431	158	
1929	do.	do.	323	89	
1930	do.	do.	477	143	
1931[1]	do.	do.	827	202	
1932	do.	do.	373	44	Bad health and consequently little fishing.
1933	do.	do.	249	31	
1934	do.	do.	504	1	

These figures show that, from 1913 to 1934, Mr. Wood himself landed 3,490 fish, to which must be added his other totals as follow:

1903	45 fish (Ireland)
1912	5 fish (Scotland)

making a grand total of 3,540 salmon, exclusive of sea trout and brown trout—to the ordinary angler a staggering figure!

It may interest my readers to give a list of sea trout caught at Cairnton during the years 1918–1934. Of the

[1] The record Cairnton season.

Dee as a sea trout river Mr. Wood said : " We have a certain amount of sea trout but they do not run big, as the nets get all the big ones; 1½ lb. is the only size that can get through, and the netsmen take all the 2- and 3-pounders. The average weight of sea trout caught in the nets is just under 2 lb. in most years."

SEA TROUT CAUGHT AT CAIRNTON

	1918	-19	-20	-21	-22	-23	-24	-25	-26	-27	-28	-29	-30	-31	-32	-33	-34
April	–	–	–	1	–	–	2	1	1	1	1	2	1	1	6	1	1
May	3	–	2	7	8	1	8	9	6	2	2	3	21	12	14	4	–
June	24	–	10	4	10	8	7	8	13	6	10	4	16	18	14	6	9
July	50	2	5	3	13	3	10	6	6	4	18	9	26	13	9	4	3
August	17	9	2	2	–	1	9	–	1	4	3	18	16	11	7	6	6
Sept.	4	–	2	–	–	1	2	4	1	3	2	3	3	3	4	–	–
October	–	–	2	–	2	3	1	4	1	–	–	3	2	–	–	–	–
Totals	98	11	23	17	33	17	39	32	29	20	36	42	85	58	54	21	19

The succeeding table is of great interest, giving as it does the yearly number of salmon of different weights for the Cairnton beat. This table runs for twelve years, and so gives a very good idea of the average Dee fish. Probably the figures will surprise those who are unacquainted with the Dee.

And what inference is to be drawn from a study of the Cairnton records ? Mr. Wood very definitely stated that, provided fish were in the pools, the condition of weather and water mattered very little. In other words, fish could be caught under any

CAIRNTON

YEARLY NUMBER OF SALMON AT DIFFERENT WEIGHTS

Year	Lbs. 2	3	4	5	6	7	8	9	10	11	12	13	14	15	16	17	18	19	20	21	22	23	24	25	26	27	28	Ttal
1920	2	3	3	36	93	189	162	82	25	16	17	8	8	11	18	8	7	7	3	3		1				1	1	706
1921		3	5	14	59	82	46	25	9	1	8	11	9	2	2	2	3	4	1		2		1	1		1		290
1922		9	6	28	77	113	68	20	20	12	11	20	18	27	30	16	17	9	9	8	6	1	2	2	2	1	1	564
1923		3	8	26	96	121	117	75	29	23	13	22	8	9	11	12	6	3	5	3	1	7	2	1	1			603
1924	5	3	8	10	32	82	71	45	24	15	6	9	8	11	11	13	10	6	6	5	1	2		1	1	1		391
1925	1	7	7	2	28	78	108	91	47	28	22	7	7	12	8	6	7	3	3	2	1	2	4	1	3	3		479
1926	1	9	2	6	91	130	94	48	20	15	5	2	4	6	5	3	7	3	4		6	2	1		3	1		505
1927		6	15	29	19	29	96	101	64	37	15	26	14	16	22	14	12	9	11	9	1	2	3	3	1	1	1	521
1928	2	3	6	1	46	87	98	45	26	19	9	7	5	11	12	10	6	5	7	3	6	5	4	4		1		430
1929	1	4	4	13	44	52	63	20	15	4	6	10	10	12	12	14	13	10	3	4	1		4	4	1	2		323
1930	3	11	5	17	38	80	92	55	10	14	21	14	16	34	9	8	12	9	4	6	3	3	4	1	1	1		476
1931		6	9	17	75	170	176	111	66	27	21	23	24	25	12	19	14	10	8	3	2	3	1	2	1	2		824
1932		1	10	20	23	44	59	54	45	24	13	13	11	11	13	11	11	4	6	10	8	5	5	4		1	1	371

BIG FISH

Year	Lbs. 29	30	31	32	33	34	35	36	37	38	39	40	41	42	43	44	45	46	47	48	49	50	Ttal
1920	1								1														1
1921	1			1																			3
1922	1			1																			2
1928						1											1						1
1930		1													1								1
1931	2																						3
1932		1																					2

conditions short of a roaring spate. Further, he did not believe that the pattern of the fly was of the least importance provided its size was correct; and presentation was the vital factor. In short, it would seem that his records prove nothing, *except that his method would kill at practically any time*. Those who seek to prove that a given set of conditions infallibly put down the fish would find small support in the Cairnton books. Dipping into them at random we find such entries as:

March 9th, 1925. A. H. E. Wood, 4 fish on Beauly 4/0½. Gauge 2 ft. 4 ins., 2 ft. 2 ins. Temperature 33°, 34°. Heavy snowstorms all the time. N. wind, strong. Grue till mid-day.

April 27th, 1925. A. H. E. Wood, 7 fish, 6 on Silver Blue No. 1, 1 on Blue Charm No. 1. Gauge, 3 ft. 7 ins., 2 ft. 6 ins. Temperature 44°, 46°. E. wind, strong. Occasional sun. Slight showers. Big black clouds.

April 19th, 1926. A. H. E. Wood, 8 fish on Blue Charm Nos. 5 and 4. N.W. wind. Gauge 11 ins., 1 ft. 1 in. Temperature 45°, 48°. Heavy thunderstorms and bright intervals.

May 7th, 1927. A. H. E. Wood, 4 fish on Blue Charm No. 7. Gauge 2 ft. 3 ins., 2 ft. 1 in. Temperature 44°, 52°. Very hot day. Big shoal of fish running all day.

May 11th, 1927. A. H. E. Wood, 8 fish, 4 on March Brown No. 8, 4 on Blue Charm Nos. 7 and 2. Gauge

1 ft. 11 ins., 1 ft. 8 ins. Temperature 45°, 50°. N.W. cold wind. Some sun. Lots of fish. Frosty morning.

A delightfully contradictory set of conditions : water rising and falling ; snowstorms ; thunder ; a hot day ; frosty morning ; black clouds ; sunny ; in fact, a fair selection of British weather ! And so the records continue, page after page, each seeming result being contradicted shortly after.

The same conclusion holds good as to flies. Pattern seems to be immaterial. Take for example the year 1927. Mr. Wood caught 158 fish ; 99 on Blue Charm, 36 on Jock Scott, 19 on March Brown, 2 on Silver Blue, 1 on Akroyd and 1 on Black Doctor. This would seem to show that Blue Charm was *the* fly. But to contradict this assumption there is the previously-mentioned story of Mr. Wood's bet, to win which he fished only with March Brown, *and took his full share of fish !*

During the last few seasons of his life he fished Blue Charm and March Brown—very seldom changing to another pattern unless in the mood for experiments, such as trying "toys" or " Redshanks " ; he had passed the stage of believing that there is a right poison for every fish, and followed the precept of the late Mr. Marryat, who said, " It isn't the fly, it's the driver."

Again, the records show that there is no best time of day for catching fish ; if the fish are there they are caught at all hours.

To sum up, therefore, it would seem that, as Mr. Wood once said: " There are very few days throughout the season on which greased line does not answer, as my fishing records can show." Here are the figures—for Mr. Wood and his guests.

Year.	Sunk Fly.	Greased Line.
1923	115 fish	423 fish
1924	105 ,,	245 ,,
1925 [1]	212 ,,	237 ,,
1926	137 ,,	322 ,,
1927	178 ,,	297 ,,
1928	191 ,,	216 ,,
1929	84 ,,	185 ,,
1930	124 ,,	288 ,,
1931	294 ,,	459 ,,
1932	141 ,,	189 ,,

These figures, for ten years, show that the greased line more than held its own as against sunk fly.

Finally, I would say this : judged from the point of view that experience is the best teacher, there can seldom, if ever, have been a more accomplished angler than Mr. Wood. Many men have not caught a tithe of the fish that he caught, although their fishing careers may have been longer. It is this great practical experience which, to my mind, gives such weight to his views, especially when to experience is allied great power of observation. I am quite confident that few anglers have given more thought to fishing problems than did Mr. Wood, and, " take him all in all," I very much doubt whether we " shall look upon his like again."

[1] An extremely cold Spring with snow and high water, followed by hot weather and low water in Summer. Record book states : " *Very high* water till June. Lot of snow, February and March."

CHAPTER NINE

THE DRY FLY AT CAIRNTON

DURING the Summer of 1925 Mr. G. M. La Branche, the well-known American salmon angler, visited Great Britain. His visit aroused the keenest interest amongst British salmon fishers, since there was a general desire to know whether the absolutely dry fly would kill in our waters as it had done in New Brunswick. The late Mr. R. B. Marston, of the *Fishing Gazette*, approached various riparian owners and lessees, and through their good offices Mr. La Branche was able to fish some of the finest waters in the country.

Chief interest, however, centred upon Cairnton. Mr. Wood had invited Mr. La Branche to fish his water, and to the angling world the occasion became one of great importance—would the dry fly beat the semi-dry, or vice versa? Unfortunately, conditions were thoroughly unsatisfactory; the prolonged drought of that Summer had left the majority of rivers in a hopeless state, with very few fish in their pools; but at Cairnton there seemed to be a reasonable prospect of success. A considerable number of salmon fishermen watched Mr. La Branche—which may have been a contributory cause of the result which followed. His impressions are given in a letter to Mr. Wood :—

As you may not remember the things which I considered operated for and against success, I am putting them down again :

Conditions of Water

In my opinion—perfect. With no knowledge of climatic conditions or the effect of barometric pressure upon the fish in your river, my first look at the Dee at Cairnton made me not only hopeful, but almost confident.

The clarity of the water, its height, the character of the streams and the positive knowledge that there were fish in the pools and runs, so ideal was everything, that I could easily have imagined that I was at home on one of our own rivers. Notwithstanding this similarity I did not lose sight of the fact that I was on unfamiliar water, or that the methods which had proved so effective in New Brunswick might produce nothing in Scotland. So, while I had solid faith in the dry fly and its ability to rise fish in almost any river, this confidence was not unmixed with a feeling of apprehension that here, on your river, the whole theory might go smash !

In a measure it did, but not entirely, as I think you will agree. You saw enough I believe to satisfy you that fish can be killed on the dry fly. Of course, your own method, not so far removed from mine, would not be the wet fly used for comparison. I am speaking of the average salmon angler using the orthodox, downstream style. I am not ridiculing this method, I mention it only because I believe that during the season it will account for as many fish as any other, if not more—barring your method— but I do think that the dry fly will kill when our grandfathers' method will not—and I am inclined to believe that you will agree with me again.

Older Fish

By this I do not mean fish that through age in the river have become sophisticated. When the comparison is made between the runs of fish in your waters and those in ours, beginning in February in your case and not until the middle of April to June 1st in ours, you will understand that in July, when I was with you on the Dee, the season approximated September on our rivers, at the earliest—and our fishing is ended then by two weeks—by law. Fish that have been in the river for some time are more difficult to move than those fresh run, and if this is so, the longer they are in the river, the smaller chance one has with them.

Whether or not the dry fly will kill on your rivers, early, is something I would dearly love to know. I am sure you will give it a real test. In May or June, with the water in normal or even sub-normal condition, I am convinced that the method will prove effective. Some of the fish which rose to the dry fly in the Ballater Water, while not exactly fresh run, were certainly not " potted " fish and should have been killed (mea culpa).

The Wind

Baffling enough in any method of fishing the high winds on the river during my stay at Cairnton absolutely destroyed any chance of placing the fly accurately—and I know you will agree when I say that placing the fly properly is most essential. It was difficult, too, with my light tackle, to place the fly on the water at all during some of the stiff gusts. At home we would have abandoned fishing entirely with the dry fly under those conditions, but I felt no desire to kill a fish except with those dry palmers ! I might not have been able to rise a fish with the wet fly, even if I had used it, but that angle didn't interest me. Stupid, is it not ? If I had killed one half or even one third of the fish which came to the fly I might now, if I thought of it at all, sit back complacently and congratulate myself and that is all there would be to it. But what does happen is that I don't sit in my easy chair, I cannot—I get up and walk around the room wondering what on earth it was I did or didn't do to miss them !

Audience

I am looking for an excuse for not having fastened to at least one of the fish. It is disconcerting to be watched as I was watched while attempting to take one of the many salmon that were lying in those two beautiful pools. *Your* close attendance meant nothing to me ; it was not confusing. With you at my elbow I knew you were studying the method closely and would be able to discover any error which I was unable to detect myself. So please eliminate yourself from the picture. But with the Scottish gentleman, the ghillies and the onlookers on the other bank, my mind was certainly not completely on my work. All this may or may not have had any effect upon the actual killing of fish, but of one thing I am certain. After rising the fish that I did without fastening to any, I would, had I been alone, have taken chances, struck and struck hard, in an attempt to hang at least a solitary salmon. If I had I would probably have smashed as I did at the Cottage Pool when no one was looking, and as I did on the Wye at Hampton Bishop when after the only fish I rose.

Whether or not I killed one of your fish is really of no importance to me. The ability to hook a fish that rises certainly has its value, and I don't mean that I could be content to go on always merely rising fish and never laying one on the bank. What I am really trying to say is that had you and I been alone on the river I feel certain that at least a brace of fish would have been killed. I might have made mistakes which you would have recognized, and your criticisms would have helped, but I felt I was apparently on exhibition when I was met at the gate, as you will remember, with the request that I might be accompanied—to say nothing of the crowd watching from the cliff! I must admit I was nervous, and while this contributed somewhat perhaps to my failure to fasten, I cannot plead it entirely as an excuse.

Lack of Practice

You will remember I told you that I had not been fishing for four years. Until I got to the Dee I had not even seen my favourite rod for four years. This inaction may have had something to do with my failure to hang a fish but I don't think so. Fly fishing is like swimming. If you do it, you always do it. My timing, perhaps, was a bit off, but I cannot understand, in the case of those fish that carried the fly completely under, why they were not hung when I straightened the line. They should have been solidly hooked.

On our rivers we don't get all the fish that rise, either. It is my opinion that when they are not hooked, however, it is not the angler's fault in all cases. My observations on the Dee led me to believe that your fish (and I saw this plainly) came at the fly with wide open jaws, but even after taking it did not close down on it. This occurred half a dozen times, and I am still unable to account for it, unless your theory of jaw dislocation is sound. As a matter of fact, this experience would lead me to believe that you had made a real discovery. I hope you have, because it will leave me a loophole to crawl through.

Hackles too Big

I cannot yet subscribe to your belief that the hackles prevent the hook from taking hold. I will not, either, because it means abandoning my theory that the fly should " ride high." This is asking too much because I lean so heavily on it. When Hutton's keeper on the Wye voiced the same opinion I was a bit shaken, but feeling that he had never seen a dry fly fished before I dismissed the matter a little carelessly. What am I to do, however, when Marston [1] writes me in a recent letter : " I am puzzled at your not hooking our salmon—have wondered if your light rod does not pull the hook in when you strike, or whether the bushy hackles act as a guard to prevent the hook taking hold, yet you hook Canadian salmon all right." What am I to do ? Set myself up as superior to you all and say you are wrong ?

Do you remember the fish we tried for in the tail of the Cottage Pool at Cairnton ? How he was moved so many times when the fly appeared over him though he evinced no desire to take ? What do you think it meant when he moved two or three times when I went above him and drifted the fly to him ?

[1] The late Mr. R. B. Marston.

My recollection is that after we had tried a dozen times or more dapping after a fashion, he settled back into his original position, dove to the bottom and refused to move. Do you think he saw me, or did he recognize the whole thing as a fraud? There was just a moment when he looked · as though he would take. This fish was teaching us a lesson, but I can't quite put my finger on it. What was your impression?

You suggest that I broke in two fish; that is not so. I did hook a grilse and had him on for an instant only, but the fish I broke in was a real salmon. In my eagerness (it was my last day) to grass just one fish I lost my head and smashed as he rose, because I struck hard and on a straight line. This fish was on the far bank and I cast *downstream* to him, and as the whole outfit straightened out he came to the fly and—I hope he has rid himself of it by now.

The other rivers I visited were absolutely impossible; the Annan was nearly stagnant . . . the Eden was nearly as bad, and the keepers told me they had picked up thirty-eight dead fish in a fortnight . . . the Wye was in bad shape also.

To this letter Mr. Wood replied:

I am still puzzling my head as to why you did not hook those fish. Watching everything very carefully as far as the line is concerned, all those fish that came at you, if they had come at my small fly would, I think, have been hooked, at any rate a large proportion of them, without my attempting to strike ; and that is what beats me as my line on the water was more or less in exactly the same sort of position as your line was. Why should your fish have rejected the fly ? The more I think about your hackle flies and your not hooking those fish it makes me think that it has a lot to do with the hackle, as Hutton's keeper says. One of the reasons that makes me think he is correct is that I tried some of the " Crosfield " light double hooks. These are very special light hooks and in using them when fishing in my downstream method I got fish on them but they never held long enough for me to tighten the line by the water ; so I came to the conclusion that if I wanted to use double hooks I had to strike immediately I saw the fish go down with it, as they simply got rid of the fly directly they felt the bulk of it, i.e., the double hooks. Might not this be the same with your big hackles ?

Now I am going to be rude at once and say that having seen those fish get the fly into their mouths and take it below the water I do think it was your fault that some of them were not killed. I say this, but at the same time I would say it of myself if it had happened to me, because I do think if any fish takes the fly it is *invariably* the fisherman's fault if he is not hooked. I have stated this fact before and it has caused me to puzzle out a method of hooking them where you want to hook them, so that although I cannot answer your question at the moment I am inclined to think that more attention must be paid to how the line is lying on the water, and that, in tightening, your strike should be made according to how the line is lying. On the top of this I am more inclined than ever to think that the stiff hackles of the fly prevent the hook getting home.

Later, Mr. La Branche returned to the charge :

While you saw that I was unable to do just what I wished to do, because of the wind, with the line and fly—you undoubtedly observed that it was quite as important to place the line in the proper current as it was to place the fly—and for two reasons :

First—to have the fly unhampered by drag ; and

Second—to enable the angler to pick up the loose line so that the whole thing would be almost taut when the fish took the fly. I did the best I could under the conditions, and as a matter of fact, I did as well as ever I do on our rivers—but as we say over here, " there was a jinx on me " and nothing went right. On our rivers I have missed twice the number of fish I rose on the Dee and dismissed any idea that I was doing anything wrong ; but we get so many rises and hook so many that a miss is always put down to the fish.

My experience on your river has given me a new train of thought because, coming as late as I did and rising as many fish as I did, I felt that if one third of them had been killed the method would have proved itself. In any event I think it is a fair conclusion that fish can be risen to the dry fly that might not be induced to look at a wet fly.

I remember one fish distinctly. It was the fish I rose in the lower pool at Birkhall when I was looking downstream and did not see the fly taken. When I did turn, the fish had taken the fly completely under, and my line was almost taut when I tried to set the hook, and yet it came away without my even feeling the fish. What was the lesson in this instance? On our rivers that particular fish would have been soundly hooked.

Is your theory of jaw dislocation even sounder than you think it is, or do you still persist in your belief that the hackles of the fly prevent the hook taking hold? I wish I could bring myself to think so, but I cannot except when I compare the taking of a fly by a salmon with the manner in which a trout takes one.

The trout not only lives in fresh water but feeds there, consequently when he takes a fly he clamps down hard on it as a rule and hooking then is a simple matter. The salmon does not suck the fly in as the trout does, nor does he close his mouth tight when the fly is taken. His jaws, or teeth, as dentists put it, do not articulate as does the trout's, so one must allow for this difference—as you do— and learn to hook the fish where one chooses, usually in the place where the hook will hold best. In your method of fishing you have been able to observe the actions of the fish as it takes the fly quite as clearly as we who use the dry fly, only you have learned that when a fish rises in one position he is more difficult to hook than if he rose in any other position.

I have not carried my fishing to such a degree of specialization as you, but I mean to do so in future; so it will be even more necessary to see that the line is in such water as will permit me to control my fly better.

We get so many rises on our rivers that we haven't felt that it was important to learn why we missed so many fish. We have discussed it, of course, but have blamed the fish for being the stupid things they are.

My experience on the Dee has changed my line of thought. I see now that, in July, under the conditions as they were when I was at your place, that to be able to say that the dry fly is really a method of taking salmon, one must kill a few fish. How is it to be done? By changing the pattern of fly? No! I cannot yet bring myself to that thought. I cannot yet abandon the thing I consider so important, the " high-riding fly." If we cut down the hackles to enable the hook to have a better chance of engaging, can we get what I consider so important? Isn't it, perhaps, our business to study from the rise of the fish just how the hooking should be done, and not merely depend upon a taut line and the belief that the fish has taken the fly well into its mouth?

You may be interested to know that on my river, the Kedgwick, in New Brunswick, this season, two of our best wet-fly men in the club lost two-thirds of their fish after having them on for a long time—long enough to know they were securely hooked. One chap told me also, that he lifted a twenty-five pound fish in the usual manner—finger in gills—and while he held it up to be photographed he felt his finger slipping slowly up to the point of the lower jaw, the flesh and bones parting until the fish fell at his feet—the lower jaw completely split. Doesn't this all sound like disintegration? And isn't it possible that if such a condition exists a fish may not be able to close down on a fly as it should—or as a trout would do—and account to some extent for our misses?

If this is so, then your belief that the hackles of my flies are really stiff enough to prevent the hook from engaging may be quite sound, but how are we to abandon these flies if, up to now, my theory is that big hackles are necessary to make the fish come up to them? Why not abandon dry fly fishing entirely and adopt your own method—so closely akin to it? And yet so different is it that you dress your flies thinly.

Mr. Wood replied :

I am greatly looking forward to seeing you in the Spring. I am having some flies made to see if there is any way of getting over those hackle flies of yours being so very solid, that is, compared with mine, as I am still puzzled as to why you did not hook any of those twenty fish that took your fly below the water ; that is, why they did not hook themselves on your fly as they do on mine. You did strike on many an occasion when as a rule I do not strike at all until I see the fish going off with my line, in fact, in watching you I absolutely failed to understand why the fish did not hook themselves without your help.

I am still sending Dr. Rushton the jaws of the few fish we catch, and the later in the year the more dislocated everything is. I sent him a jaw yesterday of a 23 lb. fresh run fish, Autumn fish. This fish was not coloured and had not been long in the fresh water. I think I am right in saying it had only three teeth in its mouth. I can't help thinking that this dislocation or lack of teeth had nothing to do with your not hooking the fish. It might have had something to do with it but not much. However, the Spring will help us to decide better than letters.

The remainder of this story lies with Mr. La Branche.

Writing to me he said :

" My correspondence with Wood was confined, I think, entirely to those letters written in 1925.

We never came to any conclusion as to why the fish were not hooked and I was never afforded another opportunity to rise so many fish.

" It is true that I fished the Dee with Wood for three or four years after my first experience, but always in July, with the exception of one season. Most of the time spent with him was occupied by me in studying his methods and perfecting my own casting and handling of the fly as instructed by him.

" I did finally kill a fish on dry fly, in 1928 (I think). This was on the Lower Ferrochs Pool on Cairnton Water. Mr. Wood's diary has a record of this . . . and the ghillie has the fly which took the fish.

" All this is unimportant except in so far as my Birkhall experience confirmed my belief that salmon can be risen to the dry fly on the Dee. It should be an easy matter to learn how to hook them. I daresay by now it has been done.

" Having learned Mr. Wood's greased line method I became enamoured of it and used it with great success in this country. It has now become extremely popular with those skilful enough to master it, and is used supplemental to dry fly fishing. Many fish are taken in Canada by both methods and when an angler has mastered control of the line and fly as invented and described by Mr. Wood, he rarely resorts to the old wet fly style of fishing.

"Of course, few men will ever equal Wood's skill, but many do well enough to kill fish, following his precept.

"I might say that I did not try the dry fly after 1925 on any river in Great Britain other than the Dee, and as I have said before, then only desultorily."

The reader will notice that Mr. La Branche became enamoured of the greased line, thereby following in the footsteps of Mr. Crosfield and many other fishermen. I find it hard to express in cold print the strange fascination which the greased line method exerts over its devotees. Further, to watch an expert fishing is to wish to follow in his footsteps. Very, very rarely have I known an angler who refused to succumb to the temptations of the greased line!

INDEX

Autumn Fishing, 133, 192
Blue Charm, 199
— Dressing, 42
" Blueshanks ", 48, 106
Branche, Mr. G. M. La, 51, 131, 138, 201
Brogues, 51
Bumbee Dressing, 43
Cairnton, 25, 179, 201
Cards, Fishing, 38
Casting, 54 *et seq.*, 71
Casts, 38
Celluloid Dressing for Flies, 45, 47, 48
Chaytor, Mr., 61
Cold Water, 77, 117
Colour Flash, 145
Coming Short, 115
Comparison between Greased Line and Sunk Fly, 64
Covering a Fish behind a Rock, 102, 155
Crosfield, Mr., 163 *et seq.*
Days when a Fish will not take, 116
Dead Water, 155
Dee, River, 179
Double Casting, 71
Downstream Wind, 108
Drag, 79

Dressing of Flies, 42
— of Line, 37
Dry Fly, 201 *et seq.*
Enemies of Salmon, 181
False Casting, 35, 71
Feathers for Dressing Flies, 76
Feeding in Fresh Water, 142, 183
Flies, Finding right size of, 109
— Greased Line, 38 *et seq.*
— Sunk, 149
Flood Water, 159
Freeing Snagged Fly, 157
Gaff, 53
Grant Oscillating Rings, 32
— Vibration Rod, 32
Grease, 37
Greased Line, Comparison with Sunk Fly, 64
Greased Line Fishing, Principles of, 63, 128
—, Time to Fish with, 110
Greasing Cast, 37
— Line, 37, 79
Green Peacock, Dressing, 44
Gut Shyness, 139
Hackles of Dry Flies, 207
Handling Loose Line, 90
Hardy, Mr. J. J., 27
Hardy, Mr. J. R., 28
Hearing of Fish, 143
Height of Water, 189
Hooking Fish, 23, 86 *et seq.*, 113
Hooks, 48, 49

Hooks, Long Shanked, 144
Jeannie Dressing, 43
Jerking the Fly, 134
Jockie Dressing, 43
Joints, Jammed Suction, 190
Kedgwick River, 213
Kilroy Flies, 44
Knots, 51
La Branche, Mr. G. M., 59, 131, 138, 201 *et seq.*
Lady Caroline Dressing, 44
Leading the Fly, 80
Lifting Line Over, 71
Logie Dressing, 42
Long Shanked Hooks, 144
Lonsdale Library Salmon Volume, 95
Loose Line, Handling, 91
Low Water, 104, 118
Mar Lodge Fly, 165
March Brown, 199
— Dressing, 43
— Salmon Taking, 183
Mending the Cast, 21, 73 *et seq.*
Microscopes, 188
" Milling ", 188
Natural Flies, Fish Taking, 183
Origin of Greased Line, 69
Oscillating Rings, 32
— Rod Rings, 32
Oxygen in Water, 131
Playing Fish, 93
Potted Fish, 105

Presentation, 83, 95, 150
— of Fly, 83
— of Sunk Fly, 150
Priest, 52
Principles of Greased Line Fishing, 63, 128
Problems of Presentation, 95 *et seq.*
Pulling the Fly, 155
Questions and Answers, *see* Index, page 146
Records, Cairnton, 179
—, Mr. Woods, 195
" Redshanks ", 48, 106
Reels, 36
Rings, Rod, 31
Rock, Fish Behind, 155
Rod, Types of, 27
—, Experiments with, 29
—, Specifications of, 31
Rushton, Dr., 214
Sailor Dressing, 44
Scale Reading, 188
Shooting the Line, 56
— Loose Line Prematurely, 59
Short Rising Fish, 115
Sight of Fish, 141
Silver Blue Dressing, 43
Sinking the Cast, 79
— Fly, 127
Size of Fly, 109
Snagged Fly, Freeing, 157
Stream, Fishing Near Edge of, 97, 156
— Far Edge of, 96, 153

Struck Ferrules, 190
Summary of Greased Line Method, 117
Summer Fishing, 104
Sunday Work, 190
Sunk Fly, 127, 148 *et seq.*
— Comparison with Greased Line, 64
Tackle, 27 *et seq.*
Taverner, Eric, 66
Temperature, 1, 123, 181
— of Water, 189
Throwing a Slack Line, 59
Time to Fish Greased Line, 110
" Toys ", 48, 107
Ugie, River, 129
Upstream Wind, 108
Wading Staff, 52
Ward, Mr. F., 171, 172, 175
Water, Height and Temperature, 189
Water Spectacles, 46
Weather and Conditions, 120
Wind, Upstream, 108, 109
—, Downstream, 108, 109
Wood, Mr. A. H. E., 17 *et seq.*